THE MEMORIES OF AN OLE GEEZER

Harvey Schultz

authorHOUSE®

AuthorHouse™
1663 Liberty Drive
Bloomington, IN 47403
www.authorhouse.com
Phone: 1 (800) 839-8640

Published by AuthorHouse 09/02/2015

ISBN: 978-1-5049-4761-9 (sc)
ISBN: 978-1-5049-4760-2 (e)

CONTENTS

CHAPTER SEVEN: SOME PERSONAL MEMORIES OF GROWING UP ON THE FARM!

AS OUR WORLD CHANGES!
AN INTRODUCTION!

That one day we may lose all technology and all modern conveniences is not only a real possibility, but many think that it's not a matter of **if**, but **when** this will happen! In case this does happen, then drawing on the experiences of those that have lived when there was no technology or modern conveniences will be helpful. *"The Memories of an ole Geezer"* is one such book that describes how they were able to live off of the land and will be helpful to survive if we lose our modern way of life!

"The memories of an ole Geezer" was not necessarily written as a *"Help book"*, but as our world changes and seeing the real possibility of our losing all of our technology and modern conveniences, then the memories and the experiences of those that had to survive by living off of the land many years ago before the technology boom, may indeed be helpful. If, or possibility when, we lose our modern way of life then we may be faced with the question of, *"How are we going to live now that our way of life has changed?"*

I am not necessarily a conspiracy theorists, however, the hand writing on the wall is clear that our world is changing and doesn't seem to be for the better! My memories are of a much different world where freedom was cherished and life was much simpler, but the older I get the more I fear that we may be in danger of losing the wonderful way of life that I enjoyed growing up in the woods of deep East Texas.

Whether you are reading this book for pure enjoyment of the memories, history and humor that it contains or if you are reading the many practical and down-to-earth things that we did to survive, I hope you thoroughly enjoy, **"The memories of an ole Geezer"**

Harvey Schultz (The ole Geezer!)

DEDICATION

I dedicate this book to my wife (Pat) who has put up with me for 54 years and is my best friend! Thanks to my son and daughter, Paul & Ashley who are both kindred spirits and also my very good friends. Lastly a thank you to Robert Lynch and Vicky Sigler for their encouragement and their help in getting the book ready for the publishers.

Harvey Schultz (The ole Geezer).

CHAPTER ONE

SOME THOUGHTS FROM
AN OLD GEEZER!

From a young whipper-snapper
to an old geezer in a blink!

You would think that seventy-two years would just drag by and take a very long time to live right? Well, actually it did. I mean it took seventy-two years! However, it seems as if it were only a short time when I was very young and it took forever for my birthday or for Christmas to get there. I think I have finally figured it out! Time worked differently when we were young, and I think that it is because God has a sense of humor!

Until you are twenty-one, time goes by so slowly that it seems like forty one and a half years long, then God's sense of humor kicks in! He pushes a *"Fast forward"* button to # one and life speeds up. Then by the time you are fifty he has, *"Fast forwarded"* you to # two or three when birthdays and Christmas seems to happen a couple of times a year. By the time you are sixty-five or so, He has you on *"Fast forward"* to # four or five, or on *"Super speed,"* so that you barely get over one birthday and another one is staring you right in the face!! So my conclusion or what I have figured out is that God puts us in some kind of a time warp, or something, as we get older.

If you don't believe me, then just ask anyone that is up in age and they will tell you the same thing! Oh they may not have discovered God's time warp theory like I have, I mean every body is not as smart as I am, but they know that there is something very strange that goes on as we get older! Of course there is still another very unlikely explanation for this phenomenon other than my brilliant conclusion and that is that we simply forget and our memory somehow becomes distorted or imperfect, but of course this is highly unlikely.

We had a family reunion recently, but it is getting so depressing to go to these events, because everybody there is getting so old! Someone did say something about looking in a mirror or some such statement as that, but I didn't pay much attention to it.

The point that I am trying to make here is that when you look back over a life lived, whatever the age, it seems so short and you wonder where all the time went! If we are not careful we can look back at our life and have a *"pity party"*. We may wonder how our life would have been different **"if"***!* We use to say when I was a boy that *"If"* was the biggest word in the dictionary! If I had a million dollars! If I could live forever! If! If! If! But there is no way to change our past, so we may as well be satisfied with it. But doesn't life pass by in a blink?

The day the earth stood still!

Did you see either of the movies, *"The day the earth stood still?"* The first one was made right after the crust of the earth cooled sufficiently for human occupancy and the last one fairly recently. They both ended with the implication that either the earth was going to be destroyed, or that we would lose all technology, power and all modern conveniences. If the later were to actually happen, it would be like going back home for me. I had been raised in the woods of deep East Texas where they had to pipe sunshine back where we lived. No electricity was available that far back in many of the rural areas at that time.

Pat, my wife and I were in a fast food restaurant recently and the employees were running around in confusion because their computers had just gone down and they could not wait on their customers. We were both enjoying the moment, but we suggested that they just write our orders down and take our money and not depend on the computers. The young waiter looked at us like we had just came from another planet, but he finally agreed to our suggestion.

After we had retired to our table to eat our breakfast, we started discussing the thought of, what if the computers all over the world suddenly went down? Then I reminded her of the movie, made right after the cave-man days, called, *"The day the earth stood still",* where everything that was electrical suddenly stopped working for about 30 minutes and the whole world was in a panic!

Just imagine what would happen if suddenly the computers all over the world stopped working and we lost all technology. It would be nothing short of total chaos! Just about everything would be shut down, there would be confusion and panic would ensue, much like the worst-case scenario that the year 2,000 or Y2K may have been. In this case the earth would nearly literally stand still!

The memories that I have of the life that I lived would very nearly describe what it would be like if this actually happened. Some of our book will be comparing the way it was when I was growing up in such a backward community to how it is today. Essentially it is about how my world has changed! Not every one my age experienced the same things as those that lived in rural areas or in very small towns. Larger towns and cities at that time did have electricity and at least some modern conveniences.

If it were not for the fact that I have witnessed these changes happening slowly over the years that I have lived, it would have been a culture shock and I would not have been able to adapt to the changes in our society. As it is, however, I have been able to learn to use many of the gadgets that have been invented to make our lives easier and more enjoyable. Some changes have been welcomed, while others have not, but I have learned, reluctantly in some cases, to live with the changing times.

Outside was the place to be!

One of the ways that the world has changed is that children have migrated from outside to being inside most of the time. I feel that one of the largest culprits that have caused this is our technologically crazed world.

When I was growing up there was nothing inside the house that was appealing to me except on rainy or very cold days (then only out of necessity) or at night around the battery operated radio listening to our favorite programs before we went to bed. The heat in the summer was unbearable in the house, since we had no electricity for cooling or even for a fan. So somewhere outside in the shade of a tree or on the creek bank fishing or better still in the creek where it was cool, was the best place to be.

The situation today is nearly totally reversed since it is normal in most homes to have adequate air conditioning and heating, so when it's hot or cold outside, then we migrate inside for comfort. This is not bad, however our youth does not spend enough of their time outside doing physical things to get the exercise they need. Another result is that while they are watching TV, on the computer or listening to music, it is too much of a temptation to munch on food and consume sugar loaded drinks. So as a result, obesity and/or being out of shape is a problem today.

On the farm growing up there were always chores in the morning such as milking the cows and feeding all of the farm animals, then we would gather around the table for breakfast before we started to school or our week-end activities. This has also changed since there are not as many chores in the morning and maybe not a family time together for breakfast.

Our society is beginning to realize that our children need more time outside and better diet and exercise programs to improve the obesity problem. Now you can see efforts in our homes and in schools to assure that our youth are outside more, however as a boy this was never a problem, because outside was definitely the place to be!

The hill keeps getting farther away!

I remember as a young man that I considered a person that was thirty years old to be over the hill, however the hill gets farther away the older I get. In fact, thirty seems very young now that I am a few times around the block past that! It is true that when a person was fifty or fifty-five, he was considered to be getting old even by adults at that time, however with the new technology and medicines, life expectancy has increased significantly.

Today folks living to be seventy, eighty or even ninety is not unusual and even folks living to the century mark is getting more common, but folks living sixty-five or seventy was rare when I was young. So you see, *"The good ole days,"* are not always *"The good ole days."* This is definitely one change that we can live with, *pun intended!*

One of the ways that has and is extending our life expectancy is early detection of health problems that can be treated and or a suggested live-style change that can prevent strokes, heart attacks and other problems as well. We also have a grasp of better diet and exercise habits that help extend life, or at least wart off problems of which past generations may have been unaware.

Just imagine what may be in store for the future generations. Life expectancy may be even greater for our grand children and great grand children. Going over the hill is surely there for all of us, but in our present generation and the coming generations the hill may be moving farther away all the time.

Just a note of interest; according to the present 2010 statistics, 49 countries have a life expectancy that is greater than that of the United States, which has an average life span of 78.24 years. Even in this enlightened age, the different societal structures have life expectancy that rages any where from 89.78 years, to 38.48 years. Simply Amazing and definitely something to think about!

What happened to the peace and quiet?

One of the most drastic changes in my lifetime is the peace and quiet that I experienced as a boy when the sounds we heard were mostly birds singing, crickets chirping, the sounds of the farm animals or even the sound of your own breathing! The kind of toys we played with and the way we entertained ourselves was much different then than what the youth of today have. There were no such things as Televisions, computers, DVD'S, CD'S; I-Pods are any of the many fancy gadgets they enjoy today. The only toys that we had we either found or made and none of them produced much noise and definitely did not talk back!

As a result our world today is filled with much more noise compared to when I was growing up in the county. Much more of our youth's time and activities are done inside and many times on constant noise making devices. It seems that this would hamper our ability to think and to be constructive.

Of course this is from an older person's viewpoint that grew up in an entirely different atmosphere and culture. Part of the time we did have a battery operated radio that we listened to at night before we went to bed and after all of our chores were completed. It allowed our imaginations to run wild as we listened to, *"Amos and Andy," "The Squeaking door," "Gun Smoke," "The Red Rider,"* and others.

I am in no way condemning our modern conveniences, because I am as guilty as anyone in using them, however I am just explaining how much our, or at least my world has changed in just a few generations. I do believe, however, that parents should insist that their children exercise reasonable use of these devises and not to have their minds continually fed with noise, but to make some time each day to experience some quiet time. Just something to think about!

From a snails pace to the jet age!

As a boy I remember how slow paced our life was compared to what it is today. Life in the country and on the farm was much more relaxed, but now it is rushed, crowded and at times even hectic.

One of the changes that I have welcomed and embraced is having Air conditioning in the hot summer days. I am not even sure how many of our modern and pampered folks could even survive the sultry hot summer days without AC now, especially older folks and the very young. Our fast-paced life, or *"getting caught up in the rat race",* however, is a change that I have not welcomed. Unfortunately it is a part of our culture that is difficult, if not impossible to avoid.

I wrote an article recently entitled, *"our lives controlled by the clock."* It is an unfortunate fact that our lives are, to some extent or another, controlled by the clock and there is not much way to live in our world to avoid this fact. If, in an instant, we lost all technology and all modern conveniences, sitting on the creek bank holding a cane pole and not worrying about what time it is, is one thing that I think I could enjoy again.

It may not have affected me as badly, if I did not remember how it used to be in the *"Good ole days."* I say this, *"Tongue-in-cheek",* because not everything in the *"Good ole days"* is necessarily better than today's world, so we must learn to accept the good with the bad.

It is quiet a change when we can send someone to the moon today, as quickly as we could ride to town and back to get groceries on Saturday in a mule drawn wagon! But having lived in both cultures and if I had the ability to choose something from the past to bring to today's world, I think that it would be a slower more relaxed life style!

Early to bed, early to rise!

I am not sure how the old saying, *"Early to bed, early to rise"* got started, but I have a good idea. When it got dark the only thing we had for lights were Coal-oil lamps and they were a little better than nothing, but not much. Their light was not sufficient for reading or doing anything around the house except right near the lamp.

Because our house had so many cracks that you could nearly throw a cat through, it was impossible to keep the bugs out that were attracted to the light. So if you did use the light to study or read by at night, you had to constantly fight the bugs. Well I guess you can't blame them. I suppose they figured that they had as much right to occupy that lighted space as anyone else, so since you had to fight the bugs to stay up, it was just as well to go on to bed!

My dad, we called him papa, bought a 25-cent western book on Saturdays when we went to town and about the only time he had to read was at night. I watched him sit right by the lamp and fight the bugs and read his book. Even though he was a very patient man, his patience would soon come to an end and would go to bed himself!

Now the *"Early to rise"* part can be explained by the flies!! The dadgum flies, I don't mean to cuss, but they seem to think that it was their responsibility to crawl on your face and wake you up at first light, even on Saturday and Sunday morning! So even if you wanted to sleep late, it was nearly impossible to do so! So both going to bed and rising early was out of necessity and not necessarily by choice.

Now the rest of the saying is, *"Early to bed; early to rise, makes a man healthy, wealthy and wise."* Well I am healthy, so one out of three is not too bad! Of course most houses today are build in such a way that you can pretty much keep the insects out and the lighting is definitely much better than the old coal-oil lamps. So we can go to bed and wake up whenever we want. Of course this is just my explanation of the *"Early to bed, early to rise"* saying!

Why—it's like magic!

Until I was a teenager, we used coal-oil lamps for light, which, at best, was ineffective in lighting the house or for providing sufficient lighting by which to read or work. However it was better than candlelight and much better than no light at all. When I lived near

Tatum and Beckville, Texas, we had to have sunshine piped into our neck of the woods (just kidding). They finally did get electricity into our rural community and we installed a few plugs and a single bulb on a wire hanging from the ceiling in each room.

I remember the very first time that we pulled the string and the light came on. My first thought was, *"How does that light work? Why--it's like magic!"* The light was so much brighter than we were used to from our lamps; the whole room was lit up! When we got an electric coffee pot, I thought you would just plug it up and coffee would come out like magic! It was a letdown to learn that you had to add water and coffee and it only perked hot water through the grounds and made coffee (my thoughts of magic were devastated).

Since that experience many years ago, the technology has advanced so much that it still seems like magic to me! How all of those new-fangled gadgets work is beyond my little pea brains ability to understand. All of the things that we have learned and have discovered may only be *"a drop in the bucket"* compared to what we may learn in the future (I'm getting a headache just thinking about it).

After descending from a mountain summit one of our group read 1 Corinthians 2:9 which says in effect that anything on earth pales in comparison to what God has prepared for us in Heaven. Do you suppose that it's superior technology in Heaven that will be like magic and will be the great appeal? I doubt that very much, but it is something to think about!

What it is like to be an introvert!

I just thought you might what to know a few personal things about the author of the articles you have been reading. Several years ago I participated in a test with a number of other folks that revealed whether we were an *"Introvert"* or an *"Extrovert"* and certainly no surprise to me, I proved to be an *"Introvert!"*

I had a dream last night that caused me to want to write this. I have realized for a long time that I do not have the social or communication skills that others seem to enjoy. When an Introvert is in a crowd, many of them often do not feel comfortable and are out of touch with what is being discussed or what is being done.

An Introvert is born that way and cannot help having Introvert tendencies any more than they can help what their hair or eye color is. One of the difficulties of being an Introvert is when you are around people that you don't know or feel uncomfortable with, it can drain your energy and you must seek to get away and be alone to renew your strength.

Being an *"Introvert"* myself, I am naturally not as outgoing as an *"Extrovert"* would normally be yet with some their problem goes much deeper than just being an *"Introvert."* When shyness or recluse tendencies accompany a person that was born an Introvert, they can be in a crowd of people and feel alone, useless and out of place!

Although I am not as bad off as someone that is extremely shy or bordering on being a recluse, I am never the less often uncomfortable in a crowd. Even though I put on a good act, yet at times it is very difficult to be able to join in on the discussions or the activities, but rather I feel totally inadequate to do so!

Often, for the persons described above, even unintentional or what they mistakenly take as criticism can be taken very personal and their feelings are easily hurt.

My guess is that an Extrovert who is at home around a crowd and can have lively and very interesting discussions about subjects of which he or she is not an expert, might find an Introvert very boring! I actually envy people that can be *"The life of a party,"* because for me, and others like me, that is very difficult if not impossible!

CHAPTER TWO

WHAT IT WAS LIKE WHEN
I WAS A BOY!

Hey it's me again, you know—the old geezer! In this chapter I wanted to tell a little about what it was like when I was a boy or a young man living in the sticks. Usually we lived in the rural areas, but we did live close enough so that we were able to go to a small town when we wanted or needed something. So below describes what it was like when we did occasionally go to town, but mostly in our rural communities, on our farm and with our neighbors.

No shoes, no shirt, no service!

We all have seen these signs in store windows and we probably all agree that this is a good thing for several reasons. In the first place, who wants to smell dirty stinking bare feet right? Plus the storeowners have the right to refuse service to what they may consider undesirable dress or behavior.

It used to be very common for men to go around without a shirt to be cooler, however, our society as a whole, see that as inappropriate today, so the common signs, *"no shoes, no shirt, no service"* began to be posted to keep the *"undesirables"* out so as not to offend their other, more etiquettely correct customers.

If this were the case when I was a boy, then I would have been thrown out of all public establishments, because we went barefooted probably at least 95 percent of the time! My feet were so tough then that I could run on gravel and it would not be a problem. Almost all the students went to school barefooted in Beckville, Texas, including some of the teachers.

Of course our society has changed a lot in this area and so have I. Today my feet are so tinder that I cannot even walk outside on grass without hurting my feet. So now I wear shoes everywhere. I also used to go without a shirt as well, but not after I got bigger. Now I absolutely refuse to take my shirt off in front of people, because people are always mistaking me for Arnold Schwarzenegger and it's rather embarrassing! (Don't laugh!!)

I am in no way judging whether this is right or wrong, because I have no opinion on the matter, but I am simply pointing out that our world has and is continuing to change! Although I still see men bare-chested, it is becoming more and more rare in our society today.

Hand-me-down clothes!

Being the youngest of nine children may have had its advantages, but it also had its disadvantages. One disadvantage was the hand-me-down clothes. I don't ever remember getting a new pair of pants or overalls growing up, because I always got all the other brothers hand-me-down clothes.

When I would ask my parents why I always had to wear patched and repaired hand-me-downs that were so loose and slouchy, they would say, *"Harvey you will grow into them; just be glad you have clothes to wear, now stop complaining and go to school!"*

It wasn't like almost all the kids in school didn't wear hand-me-downs too, but I would have like to have had just one pair of overalls that was new, fit right and looked nice! But I knew not to keep on, or to be disrespectable or I might get a taste of the *"Razor Strap"* and I would much rather wear old sloppy patched up clothes than that!

Don't misunderstand me, I loved my older brothers and sisters very much and we got along very well, but I did get a little perturbed when one of them would get some new clothes, which was actually very rare, but their old pair was given to me to wear. Some how it just didn't seem fair!

I have seen kids today tell their parents that they need new clothes, because they had already worn these two or three times and they want something new! Well big deal!! They should have had to wear their brother or sister's hand-me-downs until they would literally fall to pieces, then be handed another pair of hand-me-downs to wear and I would either have to wear them or go naked and we sure didn't want to go there!!

Oh in this land of beauty, the home of the brave and the free. Surely there must be somebody out there who can sympathize with me! Somebody, like me, who went through life with nothing to wear but hand-me-down clothes!

Flour and feed sack clothes!

I just wrote about hand-me-down clothes, but now I want to tell you about home made clothes that were made from feed and flour sack material. When I was growing up the feed sacks and flour sacks were made from very pretty material that mothers used to clothe their children with at that time.

They were usually flowery and very colorful cloth that I always thought looked kinda girlish, but mama made all the boys and girls shirts, blouses and dresses from them and we wore them to school, church or wherever. Even if the boys disapproved, we kept that to ourselves and hid our disappointment, knowing full well that if we complained that the razor strap still hung on the wall right by the dishpan.

Mind if I tell you a secret? As much as I talk about the *"Razor Strap,"* I never remember it being used on me for that purpose; however, it does make a good conversation topic. The razor strap just hanging on the wall, however, served as a deterrent for us children not to be mischievous or disrespectful or there could be some dreaded consequences!

As much as it sounds like I hated wearing these home made clothes, I really did not. First it was out of necessity, because my parents could not have afforded to buy the store bought material, plus I remember with pride wearing these because mama made them!

Today, although there are still moms that make their children's attire, yet it is from store bought material and not from feed or flour sacks any longer. I would love to find out how many of the readers have either worn or have used this material to make clothes for their family. (My address is P.O. Box 1134, Crosby, TX 77532) I would love to hear from you and to share stories about your memories as a child and to know how the world has changed for you as well.

Dishes in oatmeal boxes.

Although we did not buy many things from the store except for what we could not grow or barter for, an occasional box of oatmeal was the exception. Normally our breakfast was biscuits and gravy, or fried salt pork, however, once in a while there would be something different on the table waiting for us when we got up and we would eat whatever had been prepared for us; we just could not afford to be picky eaters, because we would be told that we either eat what was in front of us or do without!

Oatmeal was one of those rare treats in the morning and there was always a surprise in the box when it was opened. As I remember it, we always wanted mama to wait to open the oatmeal, until we could see the surprise that came out of the box. There may be a cup and saucer, a bowl, or some other dish that was packed in the box with the oatmeal.

If my memory serves me correctly, there was nothing protecting the glass from getting in the oatmeal if it had been broken or chipped, but I never remember that happening. Could you imagine that being allowed in today's safety and health conscience society?

The oatmeal dishes kept us supplied with coffee cups or bowls to use, plus we all enjoyed an occasional bowl of oatmeal for breakfast. I understand that other things such as different kinds of cereal or even certain kinds of detergent also came with dishes or some other useful items packed in with the contents. Oatmeal, however, is the only thing that I remember us getting.

Although oatmeal still is stacked on the store shelves today, you no longer have the added benefit of finding dishes packed in with the contents. Remembering this link to the past gives us something to discuss and something to think about!

Why do we sift the flour?

Each time my mother made bread, pies or anything that required flour; she would sift the flour with a fine screen sifter that you turned with your hand. I asked her one-day, *"Why do you always sift the flour?"* Her reply was, *"to make sure there are no weevils in the flour that will get into our food!"*

Many years ago they did not process the flour or other products with heat in order to kill the germs or any eggs that may have been in the wheat and occasionally there would be weevils in the flour. We thought nothing of it, because this was just one of the unfortunate facts of life at that time!

One of the results of eating the untreated food was that about once a year, most parents would give their children Calomel tablets or some other products that would kill the internal worms, parasites and germs that would build up in our bodies.

One of the changes that I actually appreciate is that so much attention is now given to assure that our foodstuff is relatively germ free and that what we eat is free of bugs or other undesirables that may accompany the product in its raw form.

I loved to get a glass of fresh milk after I milked the cow and drink it or crumble cornbread in it and eat it. I was watching a program on TV one day and they were showing, through a microscope, what the untreated cow's milk looked like. Suffice it to say that it made me wander how I could have drank raw cow's milk for years without it making me sick!

I am thoroughly convinced that there are some things that are better for us not to know and I am so thankful that I did not see that when I lived on the farm and we used fresh, un-pasteurized cow's milk. But somehow folks used cow's milk and they survived it and had done so for many years!

Lowering the quilting frame!

One of the things that were in nearly every home when I was growing up, was a quilting frame that, in our case at least, hung by ropes on each corner above my parents bed so that it could be lowered when needed, then pulled up out of the way when the quilting work was done. Making quilts was a job that was both an act of love and out of necessity. Usually it was a combined effort of mothers, daughters, grandmothers or other relatives. Many times close neighbors worked together to accomplish this much needed quilting job.

This was many times a group effort where different folks made the quilting tops and then would meet at someone's home to lower the quilting frame and finish the quilts. The backing was the first thing to put on the frame, then the batting, or a thin layer of cotton, then the quilting top. They would then use a needle and thread to loosely weave the thread through all three layers of the quilt.

One of the last things that they would do is cut and tie the threads so that it held all three parts of the quilt together, usually about an inch and a half or two inches apart. As a boy I remember helping to cut and tie these threads and then I would boast that I helped make the quilts. The last thing that needed to be done was to sew on a *"Bias"* or to sew the top, batting and back together all around the edges and then the quilt was finished.

During one of these group efforts they may complete several of these in one day. As a result of several times a year of lowering the quilting frames, the families would have enough covers to keep warm during the winter. This was a very important job that, in my experience at least, normally only the ladies did.

This is one craft that is not a lost art or that has disappeared through the years, although it may be done now out of the joy of the craft, but in the olden days it was a joy alright, but it also filled a very basic need!

When we knew all of our neighbors!

Another way our world has changed is that we have become more exclusive and independent. Where we use to know our neighbors names, how many children they had and if their dog was going to have puppies. Over the years, however, we may have lived in the same house with the same neighbors on all sides and have no idea what their names are, much less know anything personal about them.

I understand how much we all want our privacy, but the point is that this has changed. When we lived in the country at one place, our closest neighbor were the Calhoun's that lived less that a half a mile on our way to town or school. Each time we walked by their house, they would open the door or lean out a window and say hello and we would have a conversation. We would ask about Mr. Calhoun, who was night watchman at the lumberyard and about their two grown children, Charles and Inez.

They were cat people; I mean they had dozens of cats, all sizes and colors, both inside and outside their house. Mrs. Calhoun may lean out the window and say, *"How was school today? Well, ok I guess, I didn't get a whoopin. Well that's good; do you know that big gray mama cat of mine?"* well I had no idea, but I would usually say, *"Yes mam. Well she is going to have kittens in about a week!"* As we got ready to leave we would say something like, *"Well that's nice."* (Like they needed any more cats).

My point in all of this rambling is that neighbors use to take time to talk to each other. Not that some do not, however many don't and it is just one of the many changes that has happened in our culture. Perhaps we should take time to say, *"Hello and have a great day."* Maybe it could even be the catalyst to a new friend and a good relationship. Just something to think about!

Eagerly watching for the mailman!

Before the invention of the telephone, computer and e-mails the way we use to get and share information was by hand written letters! The only way we use to have to stay in touch with friends and loved ones that lived a great distance away from us was through sending our letters by way of the postal service.

The history of the postal service is very interesting and the ability and speed of sending and receiving letters evolved through the years from *"Snail Mail"* that may take a month or more, depending on the distance, to having the capability of next-day delivery by way of *"Airmail"* to almost anywhere in the world! But now, by way of e-mails, we can write a letter, push send and within seconds they can read what we had written only moments before nearly anywhere in the world! What a difference!!

Before the postal service the mail was sent by folks that may be going in covered wagons across country and may plan to travel near where their loved ones lived. So they would write a letter and give them the mail they would like to have delivered. So even though it may take months, in some cases, the letter would usually get into the hands of their loved ones. When a letter was sent over seas, the letter would be sent by ship, then by land until it finally arrived at its destination!

At one time three of my brothers were in the army at the same time and so someone made a daily trip to our mail box with an excited anticipation of possibly getting a letter from one of them. When we did get a letter, the whole family that was still at home would excitedly gather around to hear the letter read, sometimes several times! After we read all of the news in the letter, a return letter was started to give him the news at home and to answer any questions he may have asked. It may take several days to complete and put the letter in the mail box and raise the flag so that the mailman would know that we had a letter to be mailed.

Sending letters may still happen, but not nearly as much as it use to, and sending letters by mail may one day go the way of the dinosaurs and just be a memory for those that looked eagerly for news to come by way of hand written mail that they would get out of their mailboxes.

When nature called!

I know that this is a disgusting subject to discuss in an article, but this was a part of my life growing up and I am convinced that it is a part of each of our lives in one way or another! Since we had no city utilities or even running water to facilitate handling our, *"delicate waste"* in a more humane way, we did the best we could under our less than perfect conditions! Folks that lived before our civilized society evolved as it is today, had to deal with their world the best way possible. In the area of dealing with the call of nature, an outside toilet was built, with a hole dug under it to accommodate the waste and away from the house as far a reasonably possible. Some used lime to try to control the flies and the stench, while others used other means, but even in the best case the results were still far less than desirable!

Although we are all different, yet there are some things and in some ways that we are all the same. With possible rare exceptions we all desire to feel loved and accepted by our family members, schoolmates, friends or anyone in our society. Without exceptions we all need to eat and drink in order to survive and as a result of our natural bodily functions we must visit the *"unspeakable little room"* occasionally whether we want to or not!

When nature called when I lived on the farm, as it invariably did, I hated to walk the path that led to our outside facilities so much that, unless it was raining cats and dogs or it was extremely cold, I would find a reason to take a walk in the woods around our house to accomplish natures call!. This was preferable by far, than to endure the stench, (that would nearly gag a maggot) and to endure the flies of the out-side toilet. Of course it was a nice place to visit when nature called, but the stay was as short as possible and the experience was definitely nothing to write home about!

Now a little information about the outside facility that may come as a shock to most in our pampered society today. They usually consisted of what we called, *"One holers or two holers"* and some had even more, but ours was a one holer!

Although it was unhandy in the winter, as much ventilation was provided as possible, for the obvious reason! A simple privacy door with a spring to keep it closed was necessary. Of most importance there was, as I remember it, always either a Sears and Roebuck or Montgomery Ward catalogue inside that served two purposes. As you were there you would flip through the catalogue and look at the pictures or read it and the other reason---well you will just have to figure that one out!!

When I went to Romania four years in succession a few years ago, the folks that lived in the country still had and used the outside toilets, which brought back a lot of memories; not necessarily good memories, but memories of how we had to handle natures call when I was young. This is definitely something to think about!

CHAPTER THREE

SOME WAYS WE MADE SOME SPENDING MONEY!

O yes I am back again! The old geezer, you know the all-wise talented one? I thought I would fill you in on some of the ways that we made some spending money when we were growing up. Although we normally had enough to eat, money was scarce and so in order for the siblings to buy what we needed or wanted, we had to take some odd jobs to fill that need. Below are some of the ways that we earned some money for ourselves and at the same time, help our parents because they had very little cash besides what it took to get the necessary things for us to live.

Cotton picking days!

I remember hearing one preacher speak about his cotton-picking experience in his youth. He said that picking cotton, for him at least, was the worst job ever. He joked, or at least I suppose he was joking, that every time he passed cotton fields today that his call to preach gets stronger!

One of the ways we made some spending money was picking cotton for the local farmers. Once the word got around that their cotton was ready to pick, we volunteered to help. So very early in the morning the owners would drive around to all the houses with his big trailer and take us to the fields of cotton to be picked.

The owner would supply us with a large, long sack that had straps that went around your shoulders. As you picked cotton the sack would drag along behind on the ground and the more cotton you picked, the heavier the sack would become and the harder it would be to pull.

I remember some of the mothers even brought their babies and laid them on top of their sacks and would drag them along behind and occasionally would stop to tend to and feed them and then go back to picking cotton. Even thought they covered them with a diaper or cloth, it was hard to believe that the heat was not too hot for them to sleep.

You would pull the sack down the middle and pick from the rows on either side of you. When you got to the end of the rows, which seemed like forever, you would take two more rows coming back. When the sack became too heavy and hard to pull, you would take it to weigh it, record the weight under your name. You would get paid so much per every pound of cotton you picked, which was not much, so after weighing your cotton and getting a drink of water you would then return to work.

Water would also be provided at the ends of the rows and at lunchtime you would find the coolest shade you could find and eat your sack lunch and drink water. At quitting time, everyone would load into the trailer, which was partly full of cotton by this time and would take us to our homes with plans to pick us up early the next morning.

The job may last for three or four days, then he would pay us for all the cotton we picked and then we would wait on the next person that needed help on his farm. It was hot, backbreaking work and didn't pay much, but it helped give us some spending money.

Hauling watermelons!

Another way that we made some extra money when I was young was hauling and loading Watermelons in the summer for the local farmers. Some of our neighbors would have a truck coming to buy a load or two of their watermelons and they would hire us to help them.

First of all someone would go through the fields and pick the ripe watermelons, pull them off and set them in the middle of the rows for others to carry to the tractor and load them onto the trailer. The trailer would have a thick layer of hay on the bottom to protect the melons. The large truck or trucks would be waiting near by and after we had a single layer of melons, we would drive to the waiting trucks.

First we would lay a good thick layer of hay in the bottom of the truck and carefully lay our first layer of melons with some space between each melon for hay to fit between them.

We would then put another layer of hay, making sure that hay was in-between each melon or else they would bruise or burst on their trip to their destination. Each layer of melons would be loaded on the truck this way, until the driver said, "*That's enough*", and then we would start on the second truck if there was another one.

Sometimes the truckers would be hauling for someone else, however some of them would get a load for themselves and go set up at a good location and sell the melons right off their truck. In either case it would give us a day or two of work to make some spending money and I remember papa (my dad) helping also.

Although we did not normally raise watermelons, almost all of our neighbors did and they did not mind us helping ourselves to some of theirs, because many of their melons would go to waste anyway.

Hauling hay—the hottest job ever!

You didn't have to be crazy to haul hay on a hot summer day, but it helped. Hauling hay took place in the hottest and driest time of the year and as a result it was one of the hottest jobs that you could find and by far the itchiest. In a very short time, the dust and hay particles would get under your clothes and stick to you as you sweated and you would itch all day and you could not wait until the end of the day so you could go swimming in the creek or take a bath to get some much needed relief.

No part of hauling hay was easy unless you were lucky enough to drive the truck and even it was not much better. As the truck eased along those on the ground would toss the bails of hay by the two wires holding it together, to the ones on top of the trailer. They would stack the hay on the trailer and once it was full, we would ride to the barn where we would unload and stack the hay in the barn and then go back to the field for more.

When all of the hay was in the barn or at the end of the day you looked forward to two things, getting paid, which normally was at the end of each day, and the other was jumping in the creek and getting clean clothes on so you could get some relief from the heat and itching. I am not sure that the latter was not the most important thing at the moment.

Getting hay from the field to where it can be accessed for the animals is now done mostly in big round bails, which does not require handling by hand. I do see some smaller square bales occasionally, but I don't know if they are handled by hand or not, but however the hay is bailed the air is still filled with dust and hay particles.

Many of the modern tractors, however, are now enclosed and air-conditioned, which makes the hay bailing process so much better than how I remember it.

Some other odd jobs!

There were also other things we did to earn some spending money. One was to pick and sell berries to what we called city folks. But it reality they were not necessarily city folks, but country folks that just didn't want to go to the trouble of fighting the stickers, Poison Oak, getting their hands red with berry juice, having to watch for snakes or putting up with mosquitoes or other insects that accompanied this job.

I also worked for older folks to either plant or to help take care of their flowerbeds they had planted, or to work in their vegetable gardens. Our neighbors that grew watermelons and other things also hired us to help take care of their crops.

One time my brother, Floyd, (we called him Chief) got the bright idea to make a shoe shine box and go to the closest town, Wells, Texas and shine shoes for folks that wanted or needed it. It took a while to get set up in our business, but we made some regular customers and with new ones occasionally we made enough to keep us in spending money.

We would trim trees, pick pinecones, and mow yards or other things to make some spending money to go to a movie, buy candy or other things we needed or wanted.

Our shoe shine business in wells Texas!

One day Chief, my brother just older than me, came up with the really good idea of building a shoeshine box and going to Wells and shining shoes for people that wanted or needed our services. It didn't take long to see that it would be a good way to make some extra money to see movies and get some treats every Saturday.

On Saturday morning we would do our chores which were to milk the cows, feed the animals and make sure that Mama had enough water, wood or whatever else she or Papa needed for the day and then we would walk the two or so miles to town to begin our Shoe shine business. Sometimes we walked down the road to the highway hoping to get a ride into town and sometimes through the woods, which was closer but there was no chance of a ride that way, so we went to town nearly every Saturday to shine shoes.

There were usually several regular customers and then we would pick up other customers as we went down the street of Wells Texas. I say street, because there was only one street, or highway, through Wells. It was a very small town, but it did have a small movie theatre that we occasioned as often as possible.

Going to town was something that we always looked forward to, and usually it was mostly an all day event. One of the things that I remember about Wells was the many birds-nests that were in the large trees that lined the road into town. There seemed to be thousands of birds with hundreds of nests during the nesting season of the year. Of course this was the memories of a small boy!

Burn my steak to a crisp!

On two occasions our neighbor, when we lived on one place near Beckville Texas, hired us boys to come to their house and burn their dead cow! Because they were up in age and had a mentally handicapped son and had no way of moving the huge cow that had died near their home, they wanted us to come and cremate the cow where she had died. This meant cutting a lot of wood and hauling it to that location which was a lot of work and took nearly all day.

When we were asked to do this job, it was too big of a job for Shorty, Chief and I, so we asked Arlon, Jimmy,

Troy, ML and Joe, our oldest sister's children, to help us. We would make it a whole day and when the Ross' and Schultz' got together it was always a good day.

Of course this gave us an opportunity to earn some spending money and it was kind of fun to go to their house because they always made lemon-aid for us to drink and fed us as we worked. Another added benefit to helping this family was that there was a good fishing place on the *"Toomey Creek"* behind their house that only could be accessed through their land and they would let us go fishing there whenever we wished because we did work for them on several occasions.

The fishing hole behind their house was a spring fed creek and part of its origin was a spring behind our house where we lived in the *"sand hills"* near Beckville. Chief (my brother) and I tried to follow the spring behind our house, which joined other small streams that eventually turned into what we knew as Toomey Creek. We followed it for several miles and finally gave up when we realized that it was several more miles to where the fishing hole was located.

At that time there were natural springs in many locations. In fact springs were our water source at three places we lived in East Texas and the water was so good to drink. Now, however, springs are hard to find and becoming harder to find all of the time.

CHAPTER FOUR

SOME THINGS WE DID AROUND THE FARM!

Clothes washing day!

Today, washing clothes is relatively easy. Simply fill the washer with clothes and water, add detergent, and start the machine! When I was a boy, it was much different. Washday was an event that took most of the day to accomplish. Mama kept someone home from school to help her wash and any opportunity to stay home from school was great with me. I would go to any length to be the one that stayed home. I may have begged, pleaded, and said pleeeeeeese! I may have said that you may save me a terrible beating today if I can stay home and help! But she could see through all of that and tell me that it was not my turn and get ready and go to school!

If I was the chosen one and stayed home and if we were lucky enough to have caught rainwater in our tubs and buckets then it would be much easier, otherwise it meant carrying many buckets of water from the well or from the spring.

We would start a fire under the big Iron pot in the back yard to start heating the water. I would need to fill the big iron pot for washing and two #3 washtubs with water to rinse the clothes. As the water heated, we would add our lye soap to the water and then start adding clothes to the hot or boiling water.

After I had stirred the clothes, what we thought was enough, we put them into the first #3 washtub. If there was any visible dirt on the clothes, then we would use the rub board and wash them again. After we had gone through both rinse cycles we would hang them on the barbed wire fence or tree limbs to dry. All the time we would keep wood on the fire to keep the water hot. We also would replace the rinse water and refill the big iron pot for the next batch of clothes. As the clothes would dry, we folded or hung them where they went.

One of the last things we would do was to use the last wash and rinse water to give our floors a good scrubbing so that our house would be clean as well (no we didn't have carpets).

As you can see, washing then was nearly an all day event and this was why we did not change clothes until they were dirty, plus we did not have that many clothes to begin with.

After we were finished washing clothes, we would put the #3 wash tubs and buckets back under the eave of our house because we would always need water for bathing, cleaning, or maybe even our next wash day!

When an Ice Box, was truly an Ice Box!

When you didn't have electricity and had no way to refrigerate food, you had to preserve your milk and butter and other things the best way you could. The best way we had to keep food cool was in an *"Ice Box."* Even today many folks still call their refrigerators an Ice Box, because the name stuck and we continue to use it today.

When the temperature outside in the shade was 95 degrees, the milk and other things must be kept cool some way. So every Thursday a man in an ice truck came by our house and delivered a 25 or 50-pound block of ice, depending on what we needed, or more likely what we could afford that week. If we were lucky, we used some ice to make Ice Cream during the week.

As you could imagine the ice melted quickly in the hot East Texas heat, so a hole in the bottom of the Ice Box was provided for the water to run out as it melted. All too often the ice had long since melted before next Thursdays ice delivery date, so we had to come up with an alternative way to preserve our food.

I remember on many occasions, when we did not have ice, we would put our milk and or butter in a sealed container and lowered it down into our well or put it in our spring or even in the creek to keep it cool. We would take our Watermelons and put them in the creek near our house so it would be somewhat cool to eat that night and at least it kept it cooler than the ambient temperature or even in the shade of a tree.

Although this is not up to today's standards, this was the best we could do at the time and since we did not know about refrigeration we did not miss our food and drinks being as cold as we are accustomed to having them today.

Getting ready for Christmas!

Christmas was probably the biggest day of the year for us and it seemed like it would take forever to get there. One of the ways that it was different then than now is how we got ready for Christmas. A couple of weeks before, we would go to the woods and pick our tree to decorate for Christmas. Much work went into getting it ready and it took everyone to get it done.

We could not buy decorations for the tree so we made our own and one of them was popcorn strings. We would pop popcorn and get a needle and thread and make long strings to go around the tree. Then for the color red, we would gather a lot of the red Holly berries in the woods and string them up which added color to the tree.

We would go along the road and get cigarette packs that people had thrown out and we would burn the paper off and save the aluminum. We would wrap the aluminum around Sweet Gum balls and hang them on the tree.

Fresh and dry pine straw would be hung here and there to give the tree a different look. We also may find small nick-knacks or trinkets to hang on the tree as well. Decorating the tree for Christmas was a lot of the fun we had at that time of the year. Although we did not get much, what we did get meant a lot. Many of the gifts then were hand made items.

So many of our gifts for members of our family and friends were made by hand. Mama may make the boys a shirt from feed, flower or meal sack material or the girls a dress or a blouse. Some gifts may be whittled or otherwise made from wood for someone. We may have gotten mama to help us sew a Hand-Ker-chief for some of the siblings. The point is that the gifts may have been simple, but they were appreciated because they were hand made items.

Some of the "*once a year*" things that were bought for Christmas were stick candy and assorted nuts and some fruit. Mama also cooked some pies or cakes which made Christmas a very special time of the year, provided of course that we had enough money for those things. I think, however, that our getting ready for Christmas is what made it so special.

Storing our potatoes for the year!

Storing a large crop of Irish or sweet potatoes without a basement was difficult. If the potatoes were stored in a hot dry place, they would dry and shrivel up and would not be good. They would also ruin if they got wet or if they touched each other.

So on a dry day we would gather a lot of hay with our potatoes and start our stash in the hole we had dug in the side of a hill. First we would lay a deep layer of hay on the bottom of the hole, and then lay a layer of potatoes, making sure that no potatoes touch another potato. This way, if any potato was bruised and began to rot, it would not affect any of the others. Otherwise one rotten potato would eventually ruin all of the others. This is how we got the saying, *"One rotten apple ruins the whole barrel."* Once the first layer was laid, we would cover it with more hay, then lay another layer of potatoes on top of the hay and so fourth until we had stored all of the potatoes.

After the last potato was stored, we would pack as much hay around and on top of the potatoes so that the hay would absorb any moisture from the dirt and keep the potatoes dry and cool. Then we would cover the hole with dirt sufficient to where no water could get in with the potatoes.

When we chose the location for our stash, we would make sure that any water shed was away from that location, because it was necessary that the potatoes remain dry and cool throughout the year. All through the winter month's mama would tell one of the boys to go get her some sweet or Irish potatoes and bring them to her. We would then dig into the stash and get enough for her to cook and then carefully cover it up again to keep any rain from getting them wet.

As long as you kept it covered and the potatoes stayed dry, they would stay good all year or until another crop was raised that needed stored for the following year. Just something to think about!

Soap making day!

One of the several days that mama needed someone to stay home from school to help her, was when she was going to make soap, which usually took place shortly after our hog-killing day.

She would use some of the grease and lye mixed together and cook it slowly and make soap for the family to use in washing clothes and ourselves. I never could understand how you could take nasty grease and very strong lye and make a soap that you could even wash your face with! But I guess I am not supposed to understand things like that!

The great thing about soap making day was when it was my time to stay home from school, then it was a great day no matter what the occasion was. One thing about making soap that I quickly learned was that you do not stand down-wind and breathe the fumes off of the soap. It would take your breath away it was so strong.

My job in all of this was to keep enough wood cut and available and to maintain a *"low fire"* under the pot, because mama wanted the pot to barely boil or it would ruin the soap! There must have been other things that she added to the mix, but the grease and lye are the only two things I remember.

She did not add anything to make it smell good like I had heard other folks did, or any thing to make it pretty, because after it was completed it smelled very strong and kinda ugly. Did you ever hear the phrase, *"Ugly as home made soap?"* There you go!! Well I guess mama didn't think that our soap needed to smell or look good as long as it cleaned well.

Once mama thought the soap was done, she would pour it in pans, let it cool, and then cut it into blocks. The finished product was then put into containers and stored until we needed some to use. A piece of the homemade soap was always right by our dishpan on the back porch for our family to use.

Syrup making day!

The day that we were to make syrup was indeed a very big day. Much time working and planning went into getting ready to make syrup. In the spring the *"Ribbon Cane"* was planted and cared for all year. Once the Cane was ready, we would cut the Cane, remove all the leaves and then we would stack them like a teepee to keep them off of the ground. After the Cane was all cut and stacked we would load all of this on the wagon and haul and stack this close to the Syrup Mill so that it would be ready for the big day.

Another thing that we needed in big supply was wood for cooking the syrup. So a lot of time was spent cutting and hauling wood and stacking it where it would be handy to get to.

We would also need to build a Trough so that the juice could flow from the *"Squeezer"* to the cooking pan. We would make this out of 1" x 6" boards nailed together at a 90-degree angle and the length of the distance from the rollers that squeezed out the juice to the pan, which was approximately 75 feet.

The press was set up on a hill about three or four feet higher than the cooking pan. Although this was normally done by a horse on a long pole walking around and around, Minden (my oldest sisters' husband) had a tractor that he would block up in the back, remove one of the rear tires and put a long leather belt around the wheel and around the squeezer pulley, which would turn the rollers. And as we fed in the stalks of Ribbon Cane it would squeeze the juice out of the cane and send the juice down the trough to the cooking pan below.

When the big day came we had everything ready to go. Two of us boys would be on the feeding side of the cane press, and two would be on the other side to carry off all the squeezed cane stalks to get them out of the way.

As the juice ran into the cooking pan, Minden would work it very slowly through the many channels in the long pan. He would use a long push tool that fit tightly in the 4" wide channels. He would push it very slowly the length of the channel and then pull it through the next one until he went the entire length of the cooking pan.

By the time he went through the last channel the syrup would be ready to put in one-gallon cans and sealed, then start over again. It would take all day to finish this job, but we would have all the syrup that all families involved could use all year.

<u>Canning day—a family job!</u>

Whatever there was to get ready to can the next day, the family would gather on the back or front porch late in the evening and work as a family to get it ready for canning. We may have a tub full of green peas or beans to snap or hull. We could each get a bowl and set around and snap or hull and talk. There may be berries to sort and clean. Maybe a tub full of plums to sort the good from the bad, then wash them and get them ready for the next day.

When a big amount of potatoes were ready, we would need to peal and wash the larger potatoes and then cut them up and put them in clean water until the next morning so they would not turn brown overnight. If they were new potatoes we would just wash them and cut up the larger ones to be cooked with vegetables for canning stew or with green beans or peas and potatoes. We would also gather beets or cucumbers for canning pickles. Pickled beets were one of my favorite things to eat.

Another thing we may need to work on, as a family was corn. When the roasting ears were ready we would pick several tubs full and again get on the porch and start husking the ears. We would get all the silk off of the ears and wash them. Then some would get sharp knifes and start cutting the corn off of the Kolb for mama to can the next day. We would also save some ears of corn to boil for Roasting ears to eat in the next day or two.

Once we had prepared the night before what we were to can the next day, Mama and whoever was to work with her to help, would begin early while it was still cool. With no electricity, and therefore no way of cooling, we took advantage of the cooler mornings and evenings to work.

If I were helping I would make sure there was plenty of firewood for the stove and lots of water. Then whatever Mama needed to be done to help I would need to be available for that. If it were potatoes and beans to can for instance, she would start cooking them in big pans on the top of the stove or if there was enough she would cook it outside in the big pot. While it was cooking we would be boiling the jars and lids to be ready for the food later. Once the Beans and Potatoes were done, we would fill the quart jars and lightly put the lids on the jars. Then we would put the jars in boiling water for a while to finish the canning process.

After all the food that was cooked was canned in jars we would start another batch of food to cook. Once the jars finished boiling we would tighten the lids slightly and set them out to cool. All through the day as the jars cooled you would hear them pop as they created a vacuum, which meant the canning process was complete. If they did not pop, then they would not keep, so we would either save them to eat or put them back into the pot to boil again.

This may go on all day and even into the night until all the potatoes and beans were cooked and canned. As the jars cooled completely we would store them on shelves that we had built for that purpose. The next day we may be canning something different. It would be hard work and long hours, but we had to can whatever we had, or could get, so that in the winter months or when money to buy supplies was slim, then we would have enough to eat.

Time to churn the butter!

After the milk had clabbered and was ready to churn, mama would skim the cream off and add it to the contents of the churn and it would be ready for someone to churn. Actually when papa was home, he seemed to look forward to this, although I did my share of churning also. For papa, who allowed himself 10 or 25 cents a week for a western novel, this was an opportunity to read his book that he had bought on Saturday in Beckville, to sit and rest for a while without having to feel guilty for not working. The churning would usually take 30 to 45 minutes to complete.

Papa had his own way of churning. He would use his fingers to turn the plunger each time, where I would simply go straight up and down without tuning the plunger. Perhaps the way he did it did a better job of churning, but I didn't agree with that and did it the easiest and the fastest way so I could get back outside where I really wanted to be in the first place.

Occasionally I would watch papa as he would be churning and he was so engrossed in the book that he would only stop churning with his right hand long enough to turn the page and then start churning again. Mama would eventually come and tell him that he has churned long enough and that he could quit!

After the butter had risen to the top, mama would take the lid off and skim the butter off of the top, clean it and put it in a shallow pan or a butter mold to use later. The rest would be buttermilk for the family and I always love to drink buttermilk even more than fresh milk. If I happen to be the one that had to churn, I would never really be ready for the job. While churning was not hard, yet for me to have to sit still for 30 to 45 minutes was an eternity. There was too much to do outside for me to be cooped up in the house.

Milk was something that never really went bad so that it could not be used. When the milk was no longer fresh and started to turn, or taste bad, (we called it *"blinky"*) it would be set-aside for butter and buttermilk after it clabbered. You could pour the Whey off and make cheese out of the clabber, although I don't remember mama ever actually making cheese. There were ways to use the whey, but I really can't remember how we did that. We have allowed the clabber to dry somewhat and add salt and eat it like that, which was the starting of cheese.

Polk Salad greans!

One of the things that we took advantage of that grew wild in the country when I was young was Polk greens. It grew in abundance and normally grew along fence rows or at the edge of pastures and the timber line. Polk was a fairly tall, large and long leaf plant that has purple seed once it matures, but you only want the tinder leaves usually in the early stages of its growth and then usually at the top of the plant for cooking. You would need a large amount of this because it cooks down so much, so we got burlap bags (we called them toe sacks) full or a # three wash tub full for our meals.

After you picked enough for cooking, you would let it boil for a little while then pour off the water. You would then do it a second time, and then on the third time you boiled it and poured the water off, it was safe to prepare it to eat! You would add meat, salt, pepper or however you wanted to suit your taste, and then it was ready for the table. We were always told that if you didn't boil it and pour the water off at least twice that it would poison you, so we always boiled it at least two times prior to preparing it to eat.

The taste of Polk (we always called it Polk Salad) is nearly impossible to describe because there is nothing really to compare it with, because no other greens or vegetables tasted like Polk. It had a kind of wild and a strong unique tastes all of its own. I personally liked it when we had Polk Salad for a meal. Since it grew wild, it was free, but it didn't have a long season of growth, so you needed to gather it early before it matured and went to seed.

Many folks that lived in the country would take advantage of Polk and they made at least one song about this plant, entitled, *"POLK SALAD ANNIE"* and possibly more. Sadly Polk does not grow as abundantly now as it once did, but it can still be found in certain areas if you know where, when and what to look for.

CHAPTER FIVE

SOME UNUSUAL THINGS
I REMEMBER!

I miss the old smokers!

On at least two occasions when we lived between Tatum and Beckville Texas, there was a train that came right by our house. For a long time they were coal engines and a caboose at the end of the train. You could see the train coming for miles because of the smoke. Then one day there was a modern diesel engine pulling the train and we were so excited to see this modern marvel! But the next day the *"smoker"* came by again and for a year we never saw the modern train engine again.

In the winter when the caboose went by we would often wave to the man in to caboose and he would wave back! There would be smoke coming out of a stove-pipe on top because he would have a wood or coal burning heater going so that he could keep warm and would probably cook while traveling also. At night there would be a lantern lit for light hanging from the ceiling of the caboose swinging slightly as it rode over the uneven tracks! We tried to make it a point to wave to the friendly folks in the engine and the caboose, plus there were sometimes passenger cars with folks riding in the trains as well and they always seemed eager to wave as they were passing! One of the engineers would occasionally toss candy out to us as he passed, but of course it had nothing to do with us wanting to meet the train and waving at them you understand! Yeah, sure!!!!

Then one day the diesel engine came back by our house and every day after that. We kept expecting to see the old coal smokers again, but it never came back. After a while we wanted the old one back but its days were over and it was a sad day not to ever see the old smokers again. Some of the old trains are still around, but only in special situations, such as the one we rode in Jefferson Texas, but it was just a tourist attraction and a very short trip at that.

A good friend of mine that actually use to work on a train now makes trips to find the old smokers and take the rides to wherever they are going with his family. To him these are *"sentimental"* journeys that are a reminder of an age in the past that is very near and dear to him!

Let's discuss passenger trains for just a minute. When I was very young there was a passenger train that you could ride to towns that were near Beckville and evidently it was profitable for the train system to do so at that time. When cars became more plentiful, then they combined the passenger cars with the freight train, however when about everyone owned a vehicle, then even this was discontinued because it was no longer profitable to offer passenger cars for folks to use! Now about the only way you can ride passenger trains is in special rides for tourist or train lovers that seek opportunities to ride old trains and remember, as do I, the trains they saw and rode in their youth.

I had some one tell me recently that we need to forget the past and live in the present, to which I agree, however, it is difficult to forget something that has been such a very large part of your life for years. Personally there are many things in the *"good-ole-days"* that I would not want to go back and re-live, however, they are very nice memories and definitely something to think about!

Come home it's supper time!

One of the ways our families dining experience has changed is that breakfast, dinner (if not a school day) and supper, for the most part at least, the families eat around the family table. At our home, papa and mama would sit on each end and everyone else sat on the benches on each side. I know that in our more etiquettely correct society, the correct terms would be, breakfast, lunch and dinner. It may come as a surprise to you, but we did not spend much time studying the rules of etiquette in deep East Texas.

In the morning we would have to wait until our chores were done before we could eat breakfast. For supper especially, we would either hear the dinner bell that was on a pole outside, or mama would call and tell us that it was time to eat.

Wherever we were we would make our way home, because there was not a better sound in the world than that supper was on the table, because we were always hungry and ready to eat.

As we were eating our meal we would either tell or listen to what had been done or what had happened with the family members during the day. It was always a good family time where we could began to relax from a busy day and possibly discuss plans for the next day as well.

Today families have changed as to where we eat our meals or concerned, including my own. As a whole, families no longer take the time to eat around the table as they once did; instead the food is often eaten in front of the TV while watching the news, TV show or a movie.

There is nothing good or bad about change, however, it does seem that the families are missing out on a very meaningful experience by not meeting and sharing their lives around the family table. Just something to think about!

<u>My days behind the mule!</u>

This will probably come as a culture shock and some may faint dead away, but before the invention of the modern tractors, people farmed with mules, horses or even oxen. In our case we used a mule to plow our fields and work our crops. Mules were also used on Saturdays to pull our wagon to take us to town to get our much-needed supplies.

Most of the plowing behind our mule was done either by papa or one of my older brothers. I would ask occasionally when I would be able to plow, but they would usually say that I was too young, or at least too small. One-day papa said that I couldn't handle the turning plow, but I could try the middle buster.

When they turned it over to me, it was already quite late and the mule was already tired and ready go home to eat, drink and to rest! He seemed to know that I was *"new-meat"* and not big enough for the job; as a result, he had no respect for me. When I was plowing away from the house, it was all I could do to get him to make it to the end of the rows. Then as we turned, the mule would put it in high gear and I nearly had to run to keep up with him and I could not plow a straight line?

After only a short time I was getting tired and frustrated and I am sure my family was watching and probably laughing at my dilemma. After a short time I was ready to concede that I was not ready for the plow and especially the stubborn mule, so we went home! I never asked again if I could plow and so my days behind the mule were short-lived.

The more I think about it, I believe they set me up knowing what the mule would do that late in the day, so that I would understand that I, indeed, was too young or at least too small for the job. I always thought that it looked like fun to plow with the mule, but boy I found out differently. It was definitely a humbling experience and something to think about and remember!

How we survived the insect world!

Today many insects are still around, but our houses are built so that we can fairly well keep most insects out; however because of our open door and window policy (as well as huge cracks everywhere) insects of all kind were inside the house and were a part of our lives as I was growing up. One of the things I woke up to most mornings was the sound of dirt-dabbers building their homes inside our walls. They would be flying around everywhere, but we knew they would not sting if we left them alone, so that's what we did and as a result, we co-inhabited in peace.

Ants were abundant both inside and outside the house and although they were unwelcome guest inside, never the less they made themselves at home. In order to keep them from stealing our food on the table, we would keep jar lids under each table leg and as long as we kept them filled with water; it kept them off of the table and out of our food fairly well.

Although Yellow jackets and wasp were usually outside, we would occasionally pass too close to their hidden nest; someone would get stung and the war was on! Unlike the dirt-dabbers, they seem to always be spoiling for a fight and we were more than willing to accommodate them.

Flies were usually prolific and were definitely a nuisance and we had to keep everything covered with clean rags to keep them from sampling our food. While the flies were only a terrible nuisance, the cotton-picking mosquitoes, however, was a different story! We had to spank some of them, but we became blood donors to many more. We never found a way to control them, so we reluctantly had to find a way to live with them.

While these as well as fleas, which made us miserable both inside and out, there were also many other flying and crawling insects, but they were usually just a part of our outside world.

Full service stations!

The *"help yourself"* filling, stations or gas stations of today are nothing like the service stations, or filling stations, of the past. After I moved off of the farm and worked in town, one of the jobs that I had was at a full service station.

When you drove up you were approached usually by at least two people, depending on how busy they were. Immediately we would see if you needed to fill up your tank with gas. You may say, *"Fill-er-up please"* or if you were short of money you may say, *"Give me a dollar's worth Pease!"* Now how far could you go on a dollar's worth of gas today?

If you did not specify which one, then the attendant would ask, *"Regular or Ethyl?"* At that time there was no unleaded gas. While one was filling the tank, another would check your tires air pressure; clean your windows all around, unless you requested that they do not. They would raise you hood and check your oil and water and tell you if they were low. They would even take a rag or towel and wipe off any dirty spots on the car or outside mirrors.

If your oil was dirty or low the attendant would bring the dip stick on a rag to the window for you to see. He may suggest that your oil needs to be changed and If you had time, you could drive your car onto the air operated lift and change your oil at that time and unlike the one scene in Jerry Lewis's *"The Family Jewels,"* the lift would only go up so far and stop.

Then after all of this, you would pay and drive off; never having to get out of your car, unless you wanted to stretch your legs or go the bathroom, which was usually clean. With a city and state map available, they could direct you to your destination as well. Now this should bring back some memories to those that have lived long enough to experience the *"Full service station!"* and raise a lot of questions and eyebrows from the rest.

<u>Ice Cream making time!</u>

One of our favorite things to eat was Ice Cream. And on the rare occasion that we had an Ice Cream freeze, this became a very special occasion. Today we simply go to the store and get Ice Cream whenever we want and whatever flavor we want, but when I was young and on the farm, we had to make it. Mama would mix the milk, eggs, sugar and whatever else she put in the mix while we were getting things ready for the hand turned freezer.

We would put a small block of ice in a clean cloth or sack and hit it with a hammer until it was small enough to get in between the Ice Cream and the freezer container. After we put the mix into the mixer we would add a layer of Ice then sprinkle some salt on top. Then another layer of Ice, then some more salt, until it was full to the top. We would put a folded up quilt on top of the Ice cream freezer and some one would sit on top so it would not move and someone else would start turning the crank on the freezer.

As we took turns turning the crank on the freezer, occasionally we would need to add Ice and salt to keep it full. Without the salt the Ice Cream would not freeze. As the Ice Cream froze more solidly, turning the crank would also get harder. So when you could hardly turn the crank any longer, the Ice cream was done, then we started our feast of Ice Cream.

Occasionally we did not have an Ice Cream freezer and we would have to use a gallon syrup bucket in a larger container. It was much harder and took longer, but whatever it took to have Ice Cream was not too much trouble. On the rare occasions that we had Snow we would make Snow Ice Cream but then it was too cold to enjoy it as much as we would in the summer months.

Raising baby chicks in the winter?

When I was very young and although I seem to remember this, it could just be that I heard the story told so many times that I just think I remember it. My older brothers, Clarence and Johnny, had the bright idea of raising many chickens to sell or at least sell their eggs, or both, but their timing was not the best! At that time you could order baby chicks from a catalogue and they would send then by way of the postal service and they would deliver them in a box with holes for the chicks to breath and deliver them right to your door!

They had a *"Get Rich Scheme"*, and winter was not yet over, but they had thought about this and was using an abandoned empty house about a hundred yards from our house with coal-oil lamps to provide heat at night until the warmer weather arrived in the spring. Their idea was that they would get a head start by getting them early and by spring the chicks would already be half grown. What they had not planned for was an unusually cold front that came through after the chicks had been purchased and were set up in the old house, but with all of the heat they could provide, it was not enough and most of the chicks died! So much for their *"Get Rich Scheme!"*

Who knows, however, if things had worked out differently that they could have eventually been the suppliers of a large chicken restaurant chain or supplied eggs to some huge egg suppliers, then all of the phrases like, *"nothing ventured nothing gained,"* *"No guts no glory"* would have been fulfilled and they could have been successful in their winter venture!

At the very least they made a lot of memories and the story of their trying to raise baby chicks in the winter was a story that was told and re-told in our family for years and we would laugh each time it was remembered, however at that time there was probably nothing funny about loosing all of their chicks or for failing to accomplish their plans for a success in selling chickens and eggs!

Adapting to a civilized world!

There are many changes that have occurred in the little more than seventy years of living on this planet and this is just a few ways that I personally have had to adapt to a more civilized society. Although this is a personal testimony, most folks that have lived a similar length of time and under similar living conditions, have had to undergo change in varying degrees as well.

After I was a teenager the electric company finally brought power to our neck of the woods. We had electricity installed with a single light hanging from the ceiling in each room and a few plugs. I remember the first time we pulled a string and turned on a bulb. It was so bright compared to our coal oil lamp and I thought it was a marvel!

Slowly we started getting small appliances to use the electric power and the first one that I remember was a coffee pot. I thought they would simply plug the pot in and it would magically make coffee, but when I found out that you had to add the water and coffee and it just perked water through the grounds; my thoughts of magic were shattered.

It was not until I left home at 16 that I had inside plumbing and running water. Up to then we drew our water and walked a path to our outside toilet. What an uncivilized bunch of folks we were! But you know what? I have always been thankful that I was raised up in that environment, because now I can better appreciate some of the changes that have occurred and what we have today!

I suppose the greatest change is the technology boom that has happened in the years since I have left the farm and family. We had really no technology, but now it has advanced to gigantic proportions. I have actually embraced and have learned to use much of the technology that is available today.

I have considered myself to have adapted and almost have become a civilized person in our society, however, I know that some would argue that point; but it is something to think about!

Drunken chickens—a sight to see!!

As a boy I remember that one of the reasons we were able to survive was because my mother (mama) canned everything she could, which helped us have food, especially through hard times and the winter months. Rarely would we ever have a jar of canned vegetables or fruit go bad, however I remember on one occasion when one of our quarts of canned fruit spoiled, fermented and cracked the jar. Some one smelled this and walked to the edge of the woods and dumped it out.

Later that day we heard a very odd noise coming from the back yard. We looked and noticed that the chickens would suddenly start running and run into something and fall over and at the same time making the weirdest noise! They would lie on their backs, kick their legs and finally stand up and soon would start running again. First we thought that they may be sick and dying, but we discovered that they had eaten the fermented fruit and was drunk. It was one of the funniest things that we had ever seen.

We watched the chickens for a long time and laughed to see how they were acting. So if this is the way one acts when one gets drunk, then it is another good reason not to drink right? The next morning the chickens were back to normal like nothing had ever happened. (Very likely with a terrible hang-over) But it was a sight that we would not soon forget.

I have seen some very comical situations involving persons that were drunk, however the humor ends when someone you love has been seriously injured or killed by someone that has lost their ability to think or function normally because of alcohol or drugs! Many marriages have ended in divorce; businesses failed, friendships lost and lives changed, because of mind controlling substances.

Although it may not be wrong to moderately drink as long as we remain in control of our facilities, yet it is the extreme and the abuse that causes the problems. I am thankful that neither of my parents or any of my siblings had habits worse than smoking and some social drinking. I don't remember any of them *"falling down drunk,"* which is a good thing!

CHAPTER SIX

HOW WE MANAGED TO SURVIVE IN EAST TEXAS!

Having lived in the woods of deep East Texas and have experienced living before almost any technology, I have written a series of articles from my personal experience of how we survived when things were much more simple, slow paced and different conditions existed that enabled folks to live off of the land. Folks that have lived a long time and under similar conditions can probably better understand and appreciate how we lived off of what nature provided rather than what you could buy off of the store shelves.

How did folks live in such a backward society when they moved on a piece of land that was undeveloped, may not have even had access to clean water, no local doctor available, no large grocery stores to shop for food, no electricity or gas for cooling or heat, no automobiles for transportation and were as poor as church mice? This series of articles is an attempt to provide the answer to these questions.

When we lived in deep East Texas there were hundreds of acres surrounding our place that we were granted access by our neighbors for us to hunt, fish and also to look for things that grew wild that we could eat and can. By-in-large this has changed in today's society because most folks now fence their property and post "<u>No Trespassing</u>" signs so that we are no longer able to use land other than our own. So understand that our situation was different then and is one of the reasons that we were able to live off of the land!

Of course raising a garden and larger crops was a big part of how folks survived in by-gone times, however there were other things that had to be taken advantage of for folks to live off of the land. There were also other things that made the difference between going hungry and having enough food for the family to eat. Things that grew wild such as berries, grapes, plums, chinquapins, walnuts, hickory nuts, Polk salad and pecans, just to name a few, that could make a difference in a family's survival!

Wild life that use to be plentiful in East Texas were rabbits, squirrels, deer, Opossums, raccoons, wild hogs and many other things, depending on where you lived, that provided much needed meat for the family. Whenever there were ponds, creeks, rivers or lakes near were you lived; fishing could also supply the family with some much-needed food to keep a family fed.

Most farmers or ranchers also raised chickens, cows, hogs, goats, turkeys and other kinds of livestock that they could depend on to have food to put on the table or to can or in some way to preserve for winter months when food was not available as they were at other times of the year.

This article and the ones that follow will try to answer the question of how folks could survive before civilization built up and technology and modern conveniences became common to the general public. Some of the things that helped my family survive and that I will be writing about in the articles that follow may be a culture shock to the, still green behind the ears, folks that don't know what it is like to not be able to buy all you need in stores or on the internet. As you read these articles you may need to sit down or you may faint dead away, fall down and hurt yourself. So if you want to read the rest of the articles, please proceed with caution!!

Digging a well for our family!

When we moved to a new place, the very first consideration was the water source. You can have a great garden spot, good hunting and fishing, but without a good source of drinking water, these things are not enough. So the first decision to make was if there was not a spring, creek, branch or river near our place, then we had to dig a well for our water supply.

I remember on at least two occasions we moved to a place that had no water source near by, so we had to dig a well in the back yard. Once we had chosen the spot, two of us would get shovels and a pick and start a hole about three feet across and start straight down with the intentions of going down to China if necessary, to reach the much needed water.

When two was a crowd, one continued to dig, throwing the dirt out, while others moved the dirt back so it would not fall back into the hole and onto the one doing the digging! If dirt was allowed to fall on the digger, depending of course which one was digging, some well chosen superlatives or colorful metaphors would probably come out of the hole to remind us not to do that again!

When it was too high to throw the dirt out, we rigged a pulley with a rope and a bucket and after the bucket was filled, it was pulled up, emptied and let back down to be filled again. This would continue until the one in the bottom of the hole, hollered, (a good ole East Texas term) *"we've got water!!"* This may take several days to complete, but it was one of the most important considerations for our family to survive. Thankfully in this part of East Texas a good source of water was only from 15 to 20 feet deep, so it was one of the blessings of living in this part of Texas.

After we had dug and prepared the well, we built a permanent pulley system so we could have a way to draw the water and a top for the well to keep trash, dirt and the varmints out so the water would be clean for our family's use. I also remember one very hot and dry summer that the well went dry and we had to go back down and dig deeper to hit a better water source.

Today when folks need a well dug, they simply call professionals that specialize in digging wells and installing pumps to supply water for their family. This is very different from what folks had to do many years ago. However when I was in Romania a few years ago, they still had wells outside as well as outside johns, much like it was when I was young and it made me homesick for the good-old-days! (Well maybe not too much)! But it definitely brought back a lot of memories and something to think about!

Choosing and preparing the soil!

Because of the nature of my dad's work, our family moved to different locations quiet often. One of the very first things we would consider, after our water supply, was where to plant our garden and other crops. This was such an important decision because we grew much of what we had to eat plus canning some of the crops we raised for food through the winter months.

There were several things to consider. The soil needed to be the richest and best soil that we could find. If the garden spot was too low or had too much watershed, then the seed and or small plants would wash away or die from too much water at certain times of the year. It should not be too close to trees or the roots would invade our garden spot and use up the nutrients and water that what we planted would need.

Too much shade would not allow the plants to grow properly. If there were too many rocks the ground could not be worked well nor would it produce good crops. Once we settled on the best spot for our garden, we began to prepare the soil and to plant whatever crops would grow at that time of the year.

As so many things in our life, the garden and other crops needed constant care to produce a good crop. The grass and weeds needed to be pulled or dug up and harmful bugs and worms removed that would eat and destroy the tender plants. We would do what it took to keep our animals out of the garden as well as wild birds and wild animals that would steal or destroy our crops.

Tending the garden and our other crops were not number one on my list of things that I wanted to do. It probably was not even in my top ten lists, so my parents would use some convincing methods to persuade me to do my share of work and the work was more preferable than facing the methods they chose. So, given the proper motivation, I did learn to help around the farm and to do my share to provide food for the family.

There were times that we would have an exceedingly hot and dry growing season or an excessive amount of locust or other things would invade and destroy our crops. In these situations we would just have to cut our losses and do the best we could with what we had!

Raising our own food!

After we had chosen and prepared the garden spot and larger crop spots we then determined what we needed and wanted to plant. Because we grew much of what we had to eat plus canning food for use through the winter months, the garden spot was very important.

The garden was used to plant many things that did not require a large area to produce enough to eat or can, so we usually chose the garden spot closer to the house so that we could give it more attention. Because we had to raise food for our farm animals and for ourselves, then things like corn, Irish and sweet potatoes, large amounts of peas and beans and others also needed to be planted in larger plots.

Once the seed or plants were in the ground, then we needed to keep the seed watered and cared for until their root systems took hold and the plants were large enough to have a better chance to survive. Because of our limited water supply, our ability to water small or needy plants was limited, especially in the larger crops. In the hot and dry season we simply had to hope that the crops could survive until the much-needed rain came.

After the crops began to get bigger, we needed to weed the crops and to loosen the soil around the plants to aid their chances to grow properly. When the crops had matured or ripened, then the harvesting of the crops was our next priority. Potatoes needed to be dug up and canned or stored. Corn was brought to the barn and stored as well as the peanuts, dried peas and beans as well as other things that could be stored until needed.

It kept us busy through the year from planting to harvest, but it was necessary not only for our survival, but raising certain crops was also necessary to help feed our farm animals through the year as well.

Using what nature provided!

You would be surprised how many things in nature can be eaten raw, cooked, or used in other ways. Although we were by no means botanists, or experts in wilderness survival, we were, however, aware of many things that grew wild that helped us to be able to help put a meal on the table or to use in some way to help the family. These included certain weeds, bushes, trees, vines and other sources that are for the most part still available in many areas to this day!

Among the many things that we picked to eat and used in cakes, pies and candies were hickory nuts, Chinquapins, pecans and walnuts. There were dewberries, black berries, mulberries, hackberries, plums, grapes, musky dimes and occasionally peaches and pears. Most of these are still available except for the Chinquapins.

Although many of these things provided a meal, pie or cake at the right time of the year and when they were plentiful, mama also used some of these to can so that we could have food available through hard times and through the winter months when food may be scarce. I wrote about this in the next article entitled, *"Mama saved our bacon."*

There were other things that I would eat occasionally but did not bring home for the family, such as certain kind of acorns, tinder Sweet-gum leaves, and other berries that I don't know the names of and other things as well. I even ate bull nettle nuts which were actually very good. The roots are also good, but they are very deep, but if you wanted to go to the trouble to dig them up, they were very good. There were certain kinds of grasses that were eatable and what we called "Wild onions or garlic" that grew especially in the spring and in wet locations.

I have actually wished that I was a botanist and knew what all else in nature that could be eaten or used for medicine or in other ways. I think that folks in the past have eaten or used much more of nature than what we did and especially what many folks today are aware of!

Mama saved our bacon!

Although my dad, we called him papa, worked hard to bring home the bacon, it was mama that actually save our bacon! Papa did make enough to get the things that we could not grow, hunt, fish or barter for, such as salt, flour, baking powder, soda, sugar and coffee. It was mama, because of her canning everything through the year, that made it possible to have food to last through the winter months or when times were hard.

What made this especially amazing was that she did it over a wood stove in the hot summer time with no air conditioning. Just being in the house with no AC in the hot East Texas summers was bad enough, but then to build a fire in the stove and cook inside the house was even more amazing. Of course she did take advantage of the cooler mornings and evenings to do some of the canning.

She would send us kid's to gather whatever was ready at that time of the year and help prepare it for the next day. At different times of the year she would can such things as peas, beans, berries, plums, potatoes, beets, corn and cucumbers. The family would set on the front porch in the evenings and help prepare whatever she was going to can the next day.

Some of the things that we gathered that grew wild around our house and canned were Dew Berries and Black Berries. There were always plum thickets in the woods that supplied plums as well as grapes and musk-e-dines. There were also Hackberries, Huckleberries, Mull berries and some that I don't even remember what we called them. We even found old abandoned home sites where we gathered peaches and pears from the trees that they planted. These were what we used to can our jellies, jams and preserves.

Although canning was a group effort, it was mama that often faced the heat to make sure we would be able to have enough food for times when food was scarce.

One of the ways us boys were able to help was to go to places where other folks threw away their old jars and clean and sterilize them to re-use for canning our food. With new Mason or Kerr lids it saved us money to use for other things.

Don't misunderstand, canning is not a lost art, because plenty folks still can today, but mama, canning as she did, probably did as much to feed our family as what papa was able to do by working everyday. Just something to think about!

<u>Time to go hunting!</u>

I have been hunting with my family many times, but hunting was definitely not one of my talents. I remember asking my brother to let me shoot a rabbit that was standing still and not very far away. I did shoot the 16-gauge shotgun at it and sure enough there it lay close to where it was when I shot and yes it was dead, however we examined it and could not see any place that it was hit. Sure enough when we cleaned it, I had not hit it with a single shot that we could find; it must have been scared to death, which I understand is not that unusual for rabbits. That about sums it up as to my hunting ability!

All of my brothers were much better at hunting and bringing home food for the family table than me. My next to oldest brother, Johnny, had a reputation of being a successful hunter even at a very young age. In fact my parents said that if it were not for his hunting skills, that the family would have had a much harder time of having food on the table at times.

Usually our hunting trips would yield a rabbit or two and possibly a couple of squirrels. It was rare but they would bring home venison occasionally, which was always a special treat.

As thankful as we were to have food to eat as a result of hunting, yet I love to watch animals or other nature, too much to ever want to kill them. I have a great respect for life and do not want to kill anything. Occasionally my daughter, Ashley, or my wife, Pat, will call me in hysterics and say, *"Come and kill this spider!"* Well when I can I will rescue the poor thing and take it outside, If they are there, however, then they insist that I killed it so it will not get back in the house. After I smash it with something, they ask*, "Is it dead? Yes! Are you sure? Look there are body parts laying everywhere, yes its dead!!"*

I came home from a hike one day and made the mistake of telling them that I saw a rattlesnake and then I was asked, *"Did you kill it?"* After confessing that I did not! Their response was, *"Whaaaaat? You didn't kill a rattlesnake? But it was no danger to anyone! Well you should have killed it anyway."* Boy they are bloodthirsty people!! You can bet that the next time I see a snake I will just keep it to myself!

Let's go fishing!

When I was young we didn't have to be asked twice if we wanted to go fishing, because we were always ready to go! Not only was this one of our favorite things to do, but, even though we did not think a lot about it at the time, it was also a necessity. If it were not for us taking advantage of what the land provided and the benefits of the waterways as well, then it would have been harder for our family to have food on the table at times.

Fishing was an especially great treat when one of our older brothers would come home for a visit and we were able to talk them into going fishing with us. Usually when we went fishing it was on Martin creek behind our house. The creek was narrow enough so that we could set poles in the ground and let the hooks hang over into what we thought would be a good fishing hole.

Depending on what bait we wanted to fish with, determined on how long it took to set the poles out. Worms were very easy to find, but if we wanted to fish with perch or minnows, then it would require that we first fish or seine them for bait.

After our lines were set and while we were waiting for dark and the fish to bite we would select a campsite and build a fire and put on a pot of coffee. We would sit around the fire, drink coffee and start talking about previous fishing trips or enjoyable things we had done in the past. Some time after dark we would make our first trip and check all of our lines, take any fish off, re-bait our hooks and go back to camp.

If we were lucky enough to have caught some fish, then we would clean and cook what we needed for supper. We would usually have some Potatoes to cook also as well as coffee to drink. Then we would sit around and talk about the "*good ole days*" and then in a couple of hours we would check our hooks again.

We usually caught some fish while on our outing, but in our pursuit to enjoy fishing and a family outing, we also helped put food on the table for our family and thus helping us survive by living off of the land or, in this case, the water.

Our helpful farm animals!

One of our chores around the house was taking care of all of the farm animals because each one was very helpful in some way. Our mules would pull the turning plow and middle buster to help us raise crops. They also pulled our wagon when we needed to go to town to get groceries or supplies. They would haul wood for our fireplace or heater and cook stove for heat or cooking. They would haul large amounts of vegetables from the fields, but otherwise they mostly help mow and fertilize the pastures so we would have green grass.

The hogs demanded more than they gave until their unfortunate demise, then they helped feed the family. Otherwise they wallowed in the mud, eat our scraps, other kinds of hog feed and occasionally would even kill a chicken if the chickens were unfortunate enough to stick their head through the hog-pen fence. Occasionally we would find a chicken lying on the outside of the pen without a head (poor chicken)!

The chickens were very useful, both living and after their demise. One of my jobs was to find and gather their eggs for the family. The hens would try to hide to lay their eggs, but I usually could hear them cackle and fine their nests. Occasionally the hen would hid her nest so well that by the time I found it, she was setting, but we didn't mind that at all, in fact I always looked forward to watching her chicks hatch and one of the most beautiful things to me was little chicks following their mother.

One of the ways that the chickens helped was that they would help keep the snakes off of our place, eat all kind of insects, some of them off of what we planted in the garden and would also keep the tick and flea population down some.

The cows would supply us with fresh milk and butter and also an occasional calf that allowed papa to sell or trade for other things that we needed. We also had Dogs and cats around the place. The dogs helped us catch rabbits and squirrels, and guarded our place when we were gone. The cats caught mice and rats and doing so would help protect what we had stored in the barn.

These were mainly the farm animals that shared our farm and helped us survive. Today farm animals may not be as plentiful or as necessary as they once were, but we simply would not have been able to make it without them.

Hog killing day!

I know the title is very crude especially for the squeamish and the faint of heart! Perhaps I should have said something like, *"Meat preparation day"* or better still*, "Food preparation day."* However, in a real world the animal, in this case the pigs or hogs had to die for this to happen. Sorry about that!!

Today with refrigeration and an abundance of ice, preparing food is no problem. In today's world we simply go the meat department and get our choice of pre-cut and pre-wrapped meat. When I grew up and in most rural areas, however, this was not an option and we had no way to keep meat cold or frozen, so it had to be preserved to last throughout the year.

One of our big event days of the year was the first very cold day of the winter when we would have our *"Hog killing day."* We had to wait for the first very cold day so that the meat would not spoil until we had preserved it for future use. There were three main ways in which to do that and that was to salt it down, smoke it, or cook it.

Once we had slaughtered the hogs, we scalded them in a barrel so that the hair could be removed easily, because we used everything on the hog except for the hair and the grunt. After it was hung up and the internals removed, they would cut it up and place it in different piles so that we would know how to prepare the meat. Part of the hog we used to make into sausage, one part to salt down and another to be cooked or smoked.

It was truly an all day event and it help make it possible for us to have enough to eat for the rest of the year. Some would use a hand operated sausage grinder that you bolted to the edge of the table to prepare the sausage. Others would salt some of the meat and hang it in the Smoke House. The hide, or skin and other fatty parts were cut up and cooked in the big black pot for Lard and Cracklings, which was always a treat.

Because space will not permit me to go into every disgusting detail about all that was involved in this process, suffice it to say that it took us all day and usually part of the night to prepare and to preserve the much-needed meat for our family.

Except for the heart, liver and possibly a few other things, we did not process the internals, so there was a black family down the road that came and picked up all that we did not use and took it home for their use. I can not imaging, nor do I care to, how they prepared meals out of what was left. I am convinced, however, that they didn't let hardly anything go to waste. I am glad that we could at least help them, even if in a small way, because they were probably even poorer than we were and we live from one meal to another sometimes.

The bartering system worked!

One of the ways folks survived in the past was by using the *"Bartering system,"* or trading for things that they needed. The reason this system was so widely used and worked to everyone's advantage, was two fold. First most folks were poor and did not have a lot of cash to purchase what they needed.

The second reason was that normally they may raise more of one or more crops than they needed so they had enough of something by which they could barter, or trade for other things they needed. So they did the best thing to get what they needed to survive; that is they traded with their neighbors and friends.

The way it worked was if one farmer raised corn and their neighbor raised peas, then one would agree to trade a bushel of my corn for a bushel of your peas. Or I will help your build your barn if you will, in turn, help build mine. If one family had much needed quilts, then perhaps a bachelor that was unable to make quilts for himself, would offer whatever he had or even his labor for some quilts for winter.

I remember Mama making and trading one of her quilts for some much needed medicine. So when it boiled right down to it, it was providing their talents and time, to obtain what they otherwise would have to do without.

We had a neighbor that was a professional trader. He would make his rounds and get to know all the folks in the community as to what they needed and or had to trade. Then he would make a deal with folks for items at a cheap price and then either sell or trade the things that folks had a need for.

Normally the bartering system was not to make a profit, but rather trading with what they had plenty of, for something they needed and it seemed to help supply both parties with what it took to help them to survive.

This was one of the things that helped our family to have a place to live and food to eat. Papa would offer his services to a land owner that had an empty house with the agreement that he would keep up the fencing, take care of his cows and other animals to be able to live in the house and to have space to raise a garden and small crops to help us make a living.

This was a common arrangement for many folks in the rural areas at that time and it was a way both parties got what they needed and this was done normally with only a handshake and not a signed legal agreement.

Is there a doctor in the house?

Today it seems that if we get the sniffles that we go or take our children to the doctor. It was not that way when I was growing up. If you went to the doctor, then you must have been dying or they expected that you might die! There were several reasons for this. In the first place there were not that many doctors around at that time as there are today in small towns and especially in rural areas.

The second reason was that folks doctored themselves more then with home remedies, so Mama and Papa were our doctors. Another reason was that money was very hard to come by and folks could not afford to go to the doctor for just any little thing that happened. When I wrote, "*The ax and the scar*" I had cut a gash about four inches long in my leg with an ax and they used kerosene with no stitches and wrapped it with a clean rag just like they did when I nearly cut off my little toe.

It may sound barbaric, but my leg and toe healed and every sickness had a home remedy that was used with no thought of taking someone to the doctor. Don't misunderstand me, I am thankful that doctors are a little more available now and I would not want to go back to some of the home remedies that they used, but we probably don't need to rely on doctors as much as we do today.

One of the home remedies that I am really thankful that has changed is the way they treated burns. When you got burned when I was a boy, at least in my family, they put grease or lard on it, which probably did more harm than good and it did nothing to help the pain. Mama also thought that we needed a good cleaning out about once a year, so we were given Calomel tablets (I don't know if I spelled that right) and you could taste it for years with every memory of it.

Another interesting thing about doctors at that time is that they would actually make house calls, in certain situations at least. Just try getting a doctor to come to your house today!! Finally, as much as I loved my mother, I am thankful that she is no longer my doctor, no disrespect intended Mama.

Fishing on Martin creek!

One of our very favorite things to do was to go fishing and this usually meant fishing on Martin creek that flowed behind our house. This was especially fun when one of my brothers and their families came to visit and we could talk them into going fishing with us. Sometime before dark we would go to the creek and find or cut our poles for our setlines. The creek was narrow enough so that we could stick poles in the ground and let it hang over the side and it would usually be in good fishing water.

Depending on what bait we wanted to fish with, determined how long it took to set the poles out. If worms was our bait of choice, we would simply go to a spot were worms were in abundance and dig some to use that night. If we wanted to fish with perch or minnows, then it would require that we first fish for perch or seine for bait.

After we had put our lines and hooks on the poles, we would put worms, perch or whatever our bait was going to be and set all our lines in the water. While we were waiting for dark and the fish to bite we would select a campsite and build a fire and put on a pot of coffee. We would sit around the fire, drink coffee and start talking about previous fishing trips or enjoyable things we had done in the past. Some time after dark we would make our first trip and check all of our lines, take any fish off, re-bait our hooks and go back to camp.

If we were lucky enough to have caught some fish we would clean and cook what we needed for supper. We would usually have some Potatoes to cook also as well as coffee to drink. Then we would sit around and talk about the good ole days and then in a couple of hours we would check our hooks again. We would usually do this until we got sleepy or decided that the fish were not going to bite, and then we would go home to get some sleep with plans to run our hooks first thing in the morning.

Whether we caught any fish or not we usually enjoyed our outing because the family was together and we could talk and visit.

CHAPTER SEVEN

SOME PERSONAL MEMORIES OF GROWING UP ON THE FARM!

Why do we have to grow up?

When I was a young boy I could not stand to eat Spinach or Turnip greens, but now I love them. So how did the taste of these despicable things change through the years? Are there different nutrients in the soil now that make them taste different and therefore better?

I have the feeling that it is not the yucky vegetables that have changed, but rather my taste for them that has changed! As I matured many things have changed. An example is as a young boy I cared nothing about being around girls, but for some strange and unexplainable reason, at a certain age; I began to change my opinion about them!

One of the saddest days in my life was one day when I suggest to my older brother, who is a little more that two years older than me that we *"play like we are going on a great adventure."* He broke my heart when he said *"Harvey we are too old to play like."* Well he had changed, but I had at least two years of *"play like"* left in me!

Our whole life should be a process of maturing, learning and changing. Some changes may be difficult, but change or growing up is not only expected, but essential! It is not good to live in *"Never Never Land"* were you stay young forever, and we have real concerns when we see children that have difficulty maturing, whether it is mentally, physically or psychologically and in such cases it is very sad indeed.

Our Saturday trip to town in a mule drawn wagon!

Although folks that did not live in rural areas far from the nearest town may not have memories like I am about to describe, however, for most of the folks that lived in our community it was a typical Saturday!

Our most favorite day of the week was Saturday when we went to town to get supplies for the week. We would meet friends and relatives and hear all the news in their families and around town. Everyone got up early Saturday morning because there was much to do and it would be a long day. Our chores had to be done, clean up and get dressed for a long day in town. This was one morning no one minded getting all the chores done in record time so we could get started.

After all the work was done and everyone was dressed Papa would hitch the mule to the wagon and everyone would climb aboard for the several miles to town. There was a sense of excitement in the air as we began our trip into Beckville. We waved at all the people we saw that lived along the dusty road to town or that we met on the road. Us boys would drag our bare feet in the sandy road, jump off and play until we wanted to ride a while then we would jump back on the wagon. Because this would be a nearly all day event, Mama would have food prepared and of course water to drink on the way.

When we arrived at town we would see many people we knew who would also come to town on Saturdays in their wagons to get supplies and to catch up on all the news around town. We would get a nickel to spend and Papa would buy us all a soft drink. We would usually get an RC (Royal Crown Cola) because it was about the largest drink and also a "Three Musketeer" candy bar because it was one of the biggest ones. Then in the evening Papa, Shorty (Bobby), Chief (Floyd) and I would go see a movie, which sometimes would be a double feature and a cartoon. Children under 12 got in free and it cost 10 cents for adults if I remember right.

After a day of fun for everyone we would leave to get home before dark to get all of the chores done, but it would have been a great day with much to talk and to think about.

There is a dead cat in the well!

Because of the nature of our dad's work, we called him Papa, we moved around quiet a lot, usually from farmhouse to farmhouse. My dad would agree to work for a large land-owner to keep the fences up and take care of his horses and cattle and in return we would live in their farmhouse and have all of the space we needed for our garden and crops. Papa then would do other odd jobs for the landowner plus anyone else close by that needed help on their farms to earn money to buy the things that we needed.

A couple of times Papa worked at local sawmills and one time on a dairy. He would also clear land for someone that needed more land to put in crops. So In this way we would have enough money to buy the things we needed to live. As you could imagine, these kinds of jobs did not pay very well and so about all that we had money for were the things that we could not provide for ourselves.

On at least two occasions there was not a good water source at our new home and we had to dig a well for our family's use. Once the well was completed we would build a protective lid to keep the water clean and to prevent animals from falling into the well.

On several occasions the lid was left off of the well and an animal, on at least two cases it was a cat, fell into the well and drowned. Some one would come in the house and say, *"There is a dead cat in the well!"* We all knew what had to be done and no one looked forward to that. The animal had to be fished out and we would take turns drawing the water out of the well as fast as we could so that we could empty as much of the water out as possible. Then we would allow it to fill and then do it all over again until we felt that the water was pure again.

After we were finished, there would be a strong admonition given from our parents to keep the top of the well covered to prevent this from happening again. As much as we did not want to go through this again, we occasionally would leave the top unprotected. As important as our drinking water was it looked like we would be more careful, but boys being boys we had other more important things to think about, such as when we could go play or maybe go fishing or swimming. This is one of my memories as a boy and definitely something to think about!

The ax and the scar!

Because we did not have electricity, butane, or natural gas, we had to do all of our cooking and heating with wood heaters or fireplace and a wood stove. As a result one of our jobs that kept us busy, was to cut and haul enough wood to keep us a good supply of wood at all times.

Because we needed wood cut all year, one of my shared responsibilities as a boy was to make sure that enough wood was cut and stacked for our family to use for heating and cooking. One day as I was going (I was probably sent) to cut some wood, I was crossing a barbed wire fence and as I normally did, I tossed my ax over the fence, so that I would have both hands to cross it myself. However this time the handle hit the top wire in just the right way so that it bounced back and caused about a three to four inch gash to my right shin area, which ended my task of wood cutting, at least for a while.

Fortunately I was not far from the house and so I returned to get repairs done to my leg. Even today the three-inch scar is still there to remind me of what I did many years ago. Many times our mistakes and unwise decisions stay around to haunt us the rest of our lives, right?

You may be asking, *"How many stitches did it take for the doctor for such a long cut?"* Well I am glad you asked. Actually I didn't get any stitches, nor did I go to the doctor. They soaked it with coal oil or kerosene, wrapped it in a clean rag and sent me back to cut wood. What do you think I was a wimp?

One of the articles that I wrote for this series was, *"Is there a doctor in the house,"* which describes in more detail how we doctored ourselves and how rare it was for us to go to a doctor at all unless it was very serious or even thought to be life threatening. So go ahead and ask the question that I know you want to ask, *"How could we have lived in such a backward society?"*

The thing I really hated!

When I was a boy, from the time I got up in the morning, until I went to bed at night, I was active, moving, going places and doing things. The one thing that I really hated was to have to do something or to go somewhere that I had to be still! I remember that I would get out of bed in the morning and go straight outside and run around and around our house, I guess to run off some of the excess energy that had built up overnight.

We had to churn our milk when it was ready to make butter, and occasionally I would get the nod to do this chore. It was not a bad job, or even hard to do, however you did have to sit still for thirty minutes or so, but to me that was a lifetime.

Other things that I did not like were, going to school or church and squirming in my seat when I was supposed to be listening to the teacher or the preacher, what seemed to me to be forever, when there was so much to be doing outside. At age 72 and counting, my ability to sit still has improved somewhat, but not that much.

I suppose, because I could not sit still, concentrate and learn when I was a boy; it would be diagnosed as A.D.D. or Attention Deficit Disorder today. They did not know about these big fancy terms then, but contributed it to the child being mischievous or misbehaving & sometimes would blister his or her britches with one side of a paddle to get them to sit still and listen.

I have come to know my God, to love Him and His word. I read the Bible in order to know how to teach and live. But whoever wrote the song *"be still & know that I am God"* surely wasn't a person, like myself or others that are like me, where the words, *"be still"* is not even in our vocabulary.

Dusty roads and bare feet!

One of my boyhood memories is walking on roads that were mostly sand and in the hot dry summer days were dusty and very hot on our bare feet. Sometimes there may have been sparse grass along the edge of the road, but it was usually full of grass burrs, which was worse than the hot sand.

Going barefoot was both a choice, because I did not like to wear shoes, and at times a necessity, because my family could not always afford to buy shoes and we needed to make our shoes last as long as possible. In the very hot part of the day, we would run from one shade to another and when we came to a pond, we would cool our feet in the water before going on our way.

As much as I disliked wearing shoes, there were places that we wanted to go that necessitated wearing shoes to protect our feet from tons of grass burrs, bull nettles or thorns. In order to access some of our fishing ponds or other areas where the grass burrs were very thick, not to wear shoes would have been unwise indeed.

Most of the places that we wanted to go would have well trodden paths by the cows and horses that we could walk in and not be bothered by the grass burrs. The big problem was when you needed to go to places that did not have these cow trails to follow. It was then necessary to wear shoes or pay the consequences for not doing so.

Any time you left the fields and pastures into the wooded areas, the grass burrs were no longer a big problem, however you did have to keep a watchful eye on the thorns and bull nettles. If you have never had the chance to meet *"Mr. bull nettle,"* believe me one encounter would last you a lifetime, because If you ever brushed your feet or legs up against the Bull Nettle you would sting and hurt for an hour! So even though going barefooted was fun, it also had its down sides as well.

<u>Getting lost is no fun!</u>

Because where we lived presented no apparent danger as we see in existence today, my parents, even at a young age, did not mind me going about anywhere I wanted and to go exploring in the woods was one of the things I loved to do.

Occasionally I have wandered into unfamiliar areas in the woods near our home and have become lost. At first I tried to convince myself that I would come across something familiar soon and then I could find my way home, but after a long time I knew that I was as lost as I could be. At first I was very anxious, then fear set in and I hastened my steps because it was getting late and darkness would come soon! Very scary thought! Getting lost is no fun!!

We lived so far back in the *"boon-docks"* that there were hundreds of acres where you would not find a road, a fence or come across any ones house. Of course it has since grown up so that folks live closer together and more roads have been built and it is now harder to find large areas of woods like I am describing!

The goals that I had starting out for fun and adventure had suddenly been replaced with the single thought of finding my way home and to the safety of our house and my family. My family, having been concerned about me for being gone so long, would be out looking for me and calling for me. When I thought there was no hope, I would hear a faint, but familiar voice of my mother, father or one of my siblings calling my name, then I would run as fast as my feet would carry me to that beautiful voice and suddenly all of my anxiety and fears would disappear.

Anyone knows that has ever been lost, especially at a very young age, that there is no sound so wanted and welcomed than hearing your family that loves you calling for you!

It's a wonder i'm not dead!

I was visiting with one of my nephews recently (Roger Parker) who asked me if I remembered how I use to climb a tree and sway the top of the tree back and fourth until I could reach the next tree and then do it all over again! He added that I use to travel across the woods that way! Oh yes I definitely remembered it, and then I also remembered how I use to play Tarzan and swing through the woods on grape vines. I also remembered other things that I will not mention here! Boy! It's a wonder I'm not dead!!

Of all of the thousands of trees that I have climbed in my life, about the only explanation that I can give as to why I did this is that I must have been a monkey or a squirrel in another life and some of it stuck! Even at seventy and as recently as about two weeks ago (as of this writing), I climbed two trees in our yard to hang two squirrel's nest that I had built.

We would go into the piney woods and rake up a huge pile of pine straw and then we would climb up into the tree and jump from a limb into the pile of straw. To us this was a lot of fun! We would go to the barn and gather a bunch of corncobs and then pick sides and have a corncob fight. We may leave with some bruises, especially if they were wet and heavy, but we always had fun doing so!

The only reason I can come up with that has kept me alive this long is that God must protect young and innocent folks, like myself; from their stupidity while they are growing up. Plus He may have a purpose for me for which I may be unaware of and that I have been protected from disaster while I was growing up to accomplish something in my life, whatever that may be.

Looking back over my life and the many things that I have done and that has happened to me; I am very thankful that I have survived until now. I also hope that the life that I have and am living is in keeping with what my Father wanted me to do. All of this definitely gives me something to remember and to think about!

Its time for a new mattress!

The history of the mattresses and the way folks slept at night is very interesting. For many generations our ancestors made mattresses out of dry clean straw that was better than no mattress at all, but they also had un-wanted life that lived in the straw that made it miserable for the ones that chose to sleep on them. One advantage of this kind of mattress, however, was that they could wash and re-stuffed their mattresses as often as needed to cut down on the discomfort of the bugs and as long as there was clean dry straw available, it was free!

We owned and used cotton mattresses and after a year or two they would become flat and lumpy and it would be hard to find a comfortable way to sleep on them. Each person had a place that conformed to their body and even when you tried to find a new place to sleep that may be more comfortable, you would wake up back in the hole that conformed to your body. If we had been aware of the odd assortments of bugs and their eggs that lived in our mattress and probably lived on the humans that slept on the mattress, we would have been afraid to sleep in them. Thank goodness for the ignorance of such things, otherwise our lives at night would have been even more miserable!!

So it was time to re-work them and one day a man in a truck came by and picked up our mattresses and took them to their place of business to re-work them. The process of re-working the mattress was that they would take them apart, put the cotton through a process that would separate and fluff up the cotton and at the same time heat it to kill any bugs or eggs that lived in the cotton. The next step was to pack the cotton in new ducking and sew it up into, what looked like a brand new mattress. After they delivered them we were all excited that we once again had good firm mattresses to sleep on with no lumps, at least for a while!

Even though our beds and mattresses are much better today there are still critters that share our beds and spend the night with us, but they are very small and don't take up much room! So despite our unwanted guest, we just have to make the best of a less than perfect situation!

Leave the egg alone!

When I was a boy I loved to find a sitting hens nest when the chicks were hatching. It was fascinating for me to watch the baby chick emerge and often it was too much of a temptation for me not to help the chick out of its shell. To my disappointment some of the chicks that I helped out of the egg, would either not survive or would not be as healthy and strong as the others that had to struggle to get free. In the same way when the Butterfly emerges from its cocoon the struggle is necessary for them to survive.

So many well meaning parents want their children to have a better life than they had and often this means that they do not want their children to have to work as hard or to face the struggles that they had growing up. I have noticed through the years that the children who were pampered and were given everything they needed or wanted with no effort on their own did not grow up as well as those that did. Our children, like the chick and the Butterfly, need the struggle in order to be strong and to learn the value of work, money and responsibility that is required to live a happy and normal life.

We do our children a disservice when we are over-protective and do not allow them to experience at least some of life's hardships and disappointments while growing up in the home. However when they leave the nest they will have to face the world unprepared and life is a hard and sometimes cruel taskmaster. So to protect our children while still allowing them to see and experience the world as it really is, will be a blessing even though it may seem hard at the time.

I finally learned not to help the chicks out of their shell, but to simply watch them and allow them the struggle, which was necessary for them to live, and it was helpful raising our children as well. Just something to think about!

Do not touch the hot stove!

When I was growing up we had to heat and cook on a wood stove and heater and thus there was always an encouragement not to touch or it would burn. Of course, like so many children, I had to learn this the hard way! The admonition to not touch should have been enough, but once you actually touch a red-hot stove, it is not something that you would soon forget.

The way they treat a burn today has come a long way, because at that time about the only thing they seem to know to do for a burn was to blow on it, hold it in cold water and put grease or oil on the burn, which did nothing to help the pain or probably to help heal either. The old saying must be true that says, *"Time heals all"* because the burn would eventually stop hurting and heal.

There are some things in life, however, that will not heal, even with time. Many marriages end in divorce and other relationships can be destroyed by careless words or attitudes and normally time will not improve the situation.

There are harmful habits that permanently harm our minds and bodies. Even though we are warned not to drink and drive, we can cause harm to oneself or others by drinking and driving or just driving carelessly that may have consequences that are ongoing and no matter how much we regret them, we cannot undo what has been done.

As much as we may not want to listen to advice or warnings, we would be wise to pay attention to things that may have long lasting effects to our lives or to the lives of others. As important as protecting our short lives and the lives of others, yet the Bible is filled with warnings and instructions that will protect us from eternal and spiritual destruction, to which we should pay special heed. Just something to think about!

In search of a river!

When my family lived near Wells, Texas, with the exception of a few small ponds near our house, we did not have a large variety of places to fish. One weekend, some of my family was down for a visit and having heard that there was a river somewhere near us, a group set out to find it so we would have a good place to fish.

I was considered, at the time, to be too young for such a long walk, so I stayed home. When they returned, they reported that they had not found the river, however they did have some funny stories to tell that happened on the trip. One was that my brother-n-law,

Lee Parker, decided to prove that he was tough and went barefooted in what may have been one of the *"Grass burr"* capitals of Texas. About the time that they got to the barn in the pasture, he had had enough of the grass burrs, so he wrapped his feet with toe sacks or feed sacks to protect his feet.

After awhile he started complaining that the sacks were not helping, so he picked his feet up and the bottoms were completely gone and he was back to bare feet again. Despite Lee's unwise decision, he did make the trip and returned, albeit with sore feet.

Maybe one of the things that I learned from this was that we need to be as prepared as possible and not to go off half cocked when we try to find and accomplish our goals in life such as finding happiness, a soul mate, financial security or our purpose in life. Having said that, we still will need to pay whatever price is necessary to achieve them. Just something to think about!

A conversation piece!

When I was laying carpet for Persian Rug Co. in Dallas TX many years ago, we worked around home decorators on many projects. Usually, one of the last things that they would do is to lay the carpet. So we got to see many different and sometimes odd things they would used to decorate a house. Occasionally they would even use things that many would consider junk to make a statement and be a conversation piece.

One of my brothers-n-law (Lee Parker) had one of the most bazaar conversation pieces in his home that I have seen anywhere. He found a huge wasp's nest that housed about sixty or seventy wasps. He sprayed the nest, then came back later and collected the wasps and the nest and took them home. He glued the feet of the wasps and carefully put them back on the nest. Then he attached the nest above their phone in the hall, which made an interesting conversation piece. The first time I saw the nest I thought that they were alive and jumped back in surprise.

Jesus did many things that surprised His audience and I am sure that those were conversation topics for a long time afterward. Jesus did many miracles, like walking on the water, calm the raging sea, feed thousands with a boy's meal, filled two boats with fish, curse a fig tree so that it withered and died, and many other things that were attention getters. He also made statements that caused surprise in those that heard Him. Things like, love your enemies, bless those that curse you, and He used many parables, all of which would not soon be forgotten.

One of the reasons that Jesus was such a great teacher was that His method of teaching could be understood and remembered by the common person.

Even after reading the Bible for so long, I still run across things that Jesus said or did that causes awe and wonder. Perhaps more teachers could use these kinds of techniques that will create interest and provoke conversation and give you something to think about!

Drive in movies, a dionasar in intertainment.

One of the things we use to do on the weekend was go to the drive in movie theatre. Normally Minden and Laura (my oldest sister) and their family would invite us to go to the movies with them and we would all load up in the back of their pickup and go to the drive-in movie theatre near Cartage Texas. Minden and Laura would sit in the truck and watch the movie, but us boys would find a bench or just sit on the grass and watch the movie.

Occasionally you can see an old drive in movie theatre on the side of the road and there are even still a very few that are still operating today. But as a whole, they are nearly totally obsolete and will likely go the way of the dinosaurs and will be only a memory of those that were blessed to have been a part of the culture that went to watch movies at the *"Drive-in Movie Theatres"*.

Young people use to find a place in the fence and crawl under and watch the moves for free, much like we use to do at football games! I never paid to see a football game that I remember, because there were places that we knew that we could crawl under the fence to watch the games. I also remember kids slipping in with a car, because if I remember correctly they would charge so much for the cars to enter no matter how many were in the car, however some may have charged per the number of folks in the car because of the abuse of cramming so many people in one vehicle.

I also remember kids hiding from the guards and walking in besides a vehicle that had paid to come in; boy there was a lot of dishonest folks! Maybe that is one of the reasons that drive in movie theatres closed down! Many of the young folks came to the drive-in moves just to be with other kids and not necessarily to watch a move, but it was a good place to meet.

How we kept clean on the farm!

In the summer time keeping clean, at least in our opinion, was no problem; we went swimming in Martin creek nearly every evening in the summer months after we got off of the school bus. To us boys this was enough bathing for one day. Occasionally mama would give us some soap with instructions to use it while we were swimming so that we would really get clean!

Sometime we would be sent outside by our parents to stand near the well with soap and we would draw water, pour it on each other, soap up then rinse off.

We had no idea why we needed to go to such extreme measures when we had already gone swimming, but anything to please mama and papa!

In the winter time when it was very cold and we had to forgo our daily swims, we would bring a # 3 washtub by the wood stove or heater and heat water for bath time. We would hang a quilt for privacy and take turns taking a bath. Although we did not take a bath every day, when all of our arguments that we don't need a bath tonight failed to impress our parents then, they would say, *"Quit arguing, get the tub in the house and take a bath!"* For the life of us, we could not figure out why they were so unreasonable at times, but we took a bath anyway!

One day on an extremely cold day, there may have even been ice on the edge of the creek; several of us boys decided that we would go swimming so that we could brag that we went swimming in the winter. We built a very good fire, stripped down to our birthday suits, jumped in and got out as soon as we could and warmed up by the fire as we put our clothes back on. Not really a swim, but it served the purpose just the same!

Of course keeping clean now has been simplified a great deal and now we can shower or take a bath in a heated house, plus we understand now the need to take showers and baths to keep clean. Just something to think about!

Remember the old crank phones?

There were three things in our house at one time that bordered on technology. One was the old crank phone that we had for a short while when we lived on the Parkers farm near Beckville Texas. The second thing was the large battery operated radio that worked off of a large car battery, and the third thing was a wind-up Victoria record player that we used until it finally bit the dust!

When we lived in one place near Beckville, Texas there was a crank phone mounted on the wall in the living room. It was a large phone with a crank on the right side and an ear piece that hung on the left side that you put to your ear to hear. It also had a device that stood about 6" away from the phone that you would talk into to be heard by your party. You would turn the cranked to reach the party that you wanted to talk too. There were only a couple of people that we knew that had a phone that we could call and only remember one of them now and it was to the Parkers grocery store in town.

Mr. Linous Parker was the one that owned the store and hired my dad to take care of his cattle, fencing and other things and let us live in his old house with access to enough land around us to raise our gardens or larger crops that would help us have food to eat and food for our farm animals. This was something quite common for the large land-owners to do at that time that would free them up to do other things while their cattle and property would be cared for by someone that would live in an old farm house on his property.

There was an operator that would help connect you to your party, but if you knew their number you could dial it yourself. If I am not mistaken the store # was two longs and a short, which you could dial by cranking the handle twice for a few seconds and then just a second for the third dial. But every one knew your business, because it was a party line and every one could and usually did, listen in on your conversations. Boy hasn't our means of communicating changed a lot over the years?

How to carve an elephant!

We probably all have had people that have influenced our lives and that held memories that are very special to us. One such person, that influenced my life as a young boy and as I was growing up was my sister's husband, Lee Parker. I always love to visit him and to find out the latest adventure that he was into, because he was always doing and saying things that were very interesting and unusual.

I remember one job that he had was at a landfill where he would have much time on his hands. He would have soft pieces of wood and spend hours carving Pigs, horses and other things. One day, he came home with a beautiful Elephant that he had carved. I said, *"Lee how in the world do you carve an Elephant?"* He smiled and said, *"Oh that's the easiest thing in the world, just cut off everything that doesn't look like an Elephant!"* Well that was easy for him to say, but every time I tried that, I would wind up with a tooth pick.

Lee had one of the most bazaar conversation pieces in his home that I have seen anywhere. He found a huge wasp's nest that housed about 60 to 70 wasps. He sprayed the nest, then later collected the wasps and the nest and took them home. He glued the feet of the wasps and carefully put them back on the nest. Then he attached the nest above the telephone in their hall, which made an interesting conversation piece. The first time I saw the nest I thought that they were alive and jumped back in surprise.

Once Lee bought a new pair of shoes and decided that he wanted to make them waterproof and also to make them last a very long time, so he soaked the shoes inside and out with motor oil. He cleaned them as best as he could, but Lillian, his wife, later told me that after she washed his socks they were oil soaked for a long time, plus the oil compromised the thread in the shoes and they came apart very soon.

One day Lee decided to prove that he was tough and went barefooted on a long walk where grass burrs were plentiful and about the time that they got to the barn in the pasture, he had had enough of the grass burrs, so he wrapped his feet with *"toe sacks"* or feed sacks to protect his feet. After awhile he started complaining that the sacks were not helping, so he picked his feet up and the bottoms were completely gone and he was back to bare feet again. Despite Lee's unwise decision, he did make the trip and returned, albeit with sore feet. These are just some of my memories of Lee Parker, a very unique character indeed!

Why put blinders on a horse?

In past generations, farmers and horsemen put blinders on their animals to prevent them from being distracted. One day as a small boy I ask papa why he put blinders on our mule. He told me that they wore blinders to restricted their side vision and give them more of a tunnel vision on what was directly ahead of them or else they would be distracted and would not work well.

Without tractors, about the only way that folks had to plow the ground for gardens or larger crops was to use horses, mules, or even oxen, but in our case we used mules to pull the turning plows or middle busters to prepare the soil and to maintain it through the year. As I grew up and thought about what papa said about the blinders on our mule, I thought that this principle also applies to us.

I am not suggesting that we wear blinders; however in our hectic world we need more of a tunnel vision on things that are important. With our lives so crowded with so many things to think about and do, it is easy to be distracted from what is more important. This can especially affect our children, who can have so many things going on in their lives that they can loose focus on what they really need to be doing.

It is difficult to study and learn when our attention is drawn away in all directions. With folks like me whose elevators doesn't go all the way to the top and you can't think of two things at once, then we need peace and quiet to be able to think. I have, however, seen children that said that they could not think unless there was noise! Boy they need counseling bad!!

The students that seem to really learn best are those that can turn off all things that easily distracts and concentrate on the subject at hand. It is not so different for adults. Even driving has made news lately. People drive using their cell phones, eating, putting on make-up and even dressing.

The result of all of this distraction is that many accidents are caused by these kinds of activities. I heard a statistic a few days ago that drinking has gone from being the number one reasons for traffic accidents among teens and has been replaced by the use of their cell phones and especially texting while driving. Just something to think about!

How the world has not changed!

I thought, as a way to end the series of *"how the world has changed,"* would be to talk about a few ways that the world has not changed! Many physical changes have occurred such as the land filled with forest and pasture land, to now being filled with cities, towns and large suburbs.

Our population in America has grown tremendously as well as the races of people being more diversified. The greatest change, however, may be the many technological advances that have occurred during my lifetime.

In all of the previous articles I have been talking about how much the world has changed, however, it really would have been more accurate to call them, *"How my world has changed!"* As I have considered how to close out this series, I thought I would mention that although the world has changed, mankind basically has not.

There are many ways that our world has not changed. For instance, the basic needs and desires of humanity are the same. Our need for love, companionship, acceptance and fellowship remain the same. Our pursuit of fulfillment and our desire to be happy is still with us.

Although there are some stinkers and scalawags among us, yet I feel that most folks are still basically good and want to be friendly with other folks around them. Perhaps I have too much of an optimistic expectation of people, yet most of the folks that I meet from day to day, smile and are friendly when I am friendly myself and I am almost always friendly!

It has been fun to stretch my little brain to try to remember the things in my life that have changed, some I have enjoyed and some I have not. Thanks for putting up with my series of memories and what little wisdom I have accumulated along the way. I hope that they have brought back memories for those of similar life spans on our planet and have given everyone else something to think about!

Our trip down memory lane!

Although we did not exhaust the things that we could have written about how life was in the past, it did, however, end our trip down memory lane together! We may at a later date continue to write about how our world has changed, but for now I just wanted you to know that it has been fun and an honor to have written this series of articles.

I have received so many comments and compliments, deserved or not, about the memories that I have shared that I may have to buy a larger hat. I have especially had a lot of comments about, *"Dishes in oatmeal boxes,"* *"hand me down clothes."* and *"lowering the quilting frame."* I very much appreciate many of you sharing your own memories and your many comments.

I wished that I could have written this much earlier in my life to be able to touch base with so many more of the older generation that could have shared many of their memories and experiences also. I still think that there are still many folks that have memories of the things about which I wrote, or at least had it handed down to them from an older person in their life.

One of the rare times that mama shared something in their life as a younger couple, was when mama and papa were traveling in a covered wagon coming to Texas from Nebraska. They camped one evening fairly close to a farmhouse and she had cooked the very last morsel of food that they had and set it off of the fire to cool. When she turned her back later the chickens from the farmhouse were stealing their food. Mama, in hopes that she could save at least some of it, threw a stick to scare them off and hit and killed one of the chickens. The food was gone, but they now feasted on fried chicken!

Had I known what I know now, I would have encouraged, prodded and even begged them for more of their memories and stories like that. One of the things I love to do is to sit at the feet of older folks and listen to the many interesting things that happened to them and learn what it was like for them growing up. If there are older folks in your life, I would strongly encourage you to do this with them and, if possible, document this some way.

Farewell from Harvey (The old geezer)

Printed in the United States
By Bookmasters